NAMING HOW WE FEEL

NAMING HOW WE FEEL

Naming How We Feel

Specific Affect and Emotional Labor in the Writing Center

Daniel Lawson

Utah State University Press
Logan

Published by Utah State University Press
An imprint of University Press of Colorado
1580 North Logan Street, Suite 660
PMB 39883
Denver, Colorado 80203-1942

The University Press of Colorado is a proud member of Association of University Presses.

The University Press of Colorado is a cooperative publishing enterprise supported, in part, by Adams State University, Colorado School of Mines, Colorado State University, Fort Lewis College, Metropolitan State University of Denver, University of Alaska Fairbanks, University of Colorado, University of Denver, University of Northern Colorado, University of Wyoming, Utah State University, and Western Colorado University.

ISBN: 978-1-64642-862-5 (hardcover)
ISBN: 978-1-64642-863-2 (paperback)
ISBN: 978-1-64642-864-9 (ePUB)
ISBN: 978-1-64642-914-1 (PDF)
https://doi.org/10.7330/9781646428649

Library of Congress Cataloging-in-Publication Data

Names: Lawson, Daniel, 1976– author.
Title: Naming how we feel : specific affect and emotional labor in the writing center / Daniel Lawson.
Description: Logan : Utah State University Press, [2026] | Includes bibliographical references and index.
Identifiers: LCCN 2026020437 (print) | LCCN 2026020438 (ebook) | ISBN 9781646428625 (hardcover) | ISBN 9781646428632 (paperback) | ISBN 9781646428649 (epub) | ISBN 9781646429141 (pdf)
Subjects: LCSH: Emotional intelligence—Study and teaching (Higher) | Affect (Psychology)—Study and teaching (Higher) | English language—Rhetoric—Study and teaching (Higher) | Writing centers.
Classification: LCC BF576 b. L39 2026 (print) | LCC BF576 b. L39 2026 (ebook)
LC record available at https://lccn.loc.gov/2026020437
LC ebook record available at https://lccn.loc.gov/2026020438

The University Press of Colorado gratefully acknowledges the support of Central Michigan University toward the publication of this volume.

Cover illustration by Awit Enggal / Shutterstock.

Contents

Acknowledgments   ix

Introduction: Emotions Versus Affect, Labor
Versus Work, Bodies and Genre   3

1.   Developing Specific Affect Codes for Writing Center Contexts   22

2.   Affect, Collaboration, and Authority   42

3.   Burnout, Guilt, and Cynicism in the Writing Center   61

4.   Training Tutors for Emotional Literacy   89

Conclusion: More Than Just Our Centers   111

Appendix A: Modified SPAFF Codes   123
Appendix B: Modified SPAFF Handout   137
Appendix C: Emotional Labor Focus Group Interview Script   141
References   145
Index   155
About the Author   159

Acknowledgments

I would like to acknowledge the staff of Utah State University Press for their tireless efforts at helping me see this manuscript through to completion. This includes (but is not limited to) Beth Svinarich, Dan Pratt, Laura Furney, and Jennie Swanson. I am especially grateful to Rachel Levay, Skylar Cooper, and Michelle Chen. I'm also thankful for the reviewers who held my feet to the fire when I needed it but who also saw (and believed in) the promise of the project.

I thank the wonderful students and consultants at Central Michigan University. You have taught me so much, and I appreciate your contributions to this work. Several of my former students and consultants have their fingerprints on this manuscript: Hunter Tuinstra, Jimmy Hollenbeck, Faith Jacobs, Seth Glover, Kristin Brennan, and Grace Gallagher all played active roles in making this research happen. Similarly, the associate directors with whom I've worked have helped make this book possible. Emily Pioszak and Lori Rogers worked hard to make sure that we could include consultants in the research and helped train them based on what we learned. But they also kept that work from disrupting the center's vital function as a place for writers first.

I'm especially grateful for the friends and colleagues who have read drafts, offered feedback, and offered vital emotional support as I navigated the process. Jennifer Grouling-Snider and Tim Lockridge were crucial in the early

https://doi.org/10.7330/9781646428649.c000a

drafts of this book as great readers and better friends. Dana Driscoll and Genie Giaimo helped me adapt reviewer suggestions and talked me through a lot of the hardest part of the process—revision and development—after years of work. Genie especially pressed me to finish. I am grateful to you. I'm also thankful for my friends and colleagues in MiWCA, ECWCA, and IWCA. They have been there for me with enthusiasm, curiosity, and camaraderie. I look forward to every opportunity to catch up with and learn from them.

Finally, I'm eternally grateful to my family. Kelly, Jess, and Brian, you are my *why*.

Naming How We Feel

Emotions Versus Affect, Labor Versus Work, Bodies and Genre

My current writing center offers what we call "permanent appointments": one-credit workshop courses available for students at my institution. Basically, these workshop courses guarantee students a weekly appointment at the center with the same consultant each time for that semester. One of those workshop credits is a corequisite to our alternative freshman composition course, English 103. Unlike the other workshop credits we offer, this weekly appointment is dedicated specifically to the work of English 103. We often schedule new consultants in our training practicum with English 103 appointments for a few reasons. For instance, because ENG 103 students are generally first-year students, they are almost always new to college, which helps allay tutor worries about their own inexperience. More important, however, we have found that working with the same students each week has more profound effects on tutors. For example, new tutors see the development of those writers over the course of a semester, which enables them to feel some sort of self-efficacy. It also enables tutors to see which pedagogical approaches work with a certain writer over time and which do not. Tutors can also see how approaches that seem successful with some writers over time may not work with others, so they may become more sensitive to the needs of individual writers. Finally, they begin to understand the necessity of developing a rapport with these writers:

https://doi.org/10.7330/9781646428649.c000b

having to work with the same writer over the course of 16 weeks requires a great deal of such rapport to be even comfortable (let alone productive) for either party.

During my first semester teaching the writing center practicum course, one of the new tutors began complaining regularly about a student with whom she worked. This student was in one of the permanent appointments for ENG 103 and a member of the school's baseball team. In her weekly practicum journals and in her class discussions, the tutor would cast this young man as a "resistant writer," drawing on the descriptions of such from the *Bedford Guide for Writing Tutors*. She would explain that she did everything in the book—focusing on global issues, asking open-ended questions, encouraging him to take ownership of the session—but nothing would sway him. Her classmates and I would listen, attempt to puzzle out his motives, suggest alternatives, and look through the book to help her strategize. Typically, however, she would report more of the same the following week.

Ironically, I found her to be somewhat resistant to my own efforts as her teacher: She rarely incorporated the feedback I offered her in her revisions of the major writing assignments, she was dismissive of the suggestions her peers and I offered during class discussions, and she didn't seem to attempt any of the methods I suggested in her weekly practicum journals. In fact, she also continued several practices I tried to discourage. As chance would have it, she was out sick one day. Lacking anyone else to cover for one of her appointments, I covered it. The appointment turned out to be with the ostensibly resistant writer.

I greeted him and apologized for the inconvenience of working with someone other than his regular tutor. He was courteous if somewhat aloof. His work that week was for a "problem/solution" assignment for English 103. The assignment was standard for the course: Writers identify a problem or concern they are experiencing, research it, and identify potential solutions. Many chose issues common to first-semester freshman: dealing with ADHD, insomnia, budgeting as a college student, and so on. And as we began the session, I could see the basis for some of my tutor's concerns. The young man seemed unprepared, reluctant to offer full responses to my questions, and unable to respond to some of the prompts. He claimed he didn't know what to write about—that he couldn't identify any problems.

Rather than doing more of the same—and I suspect many writing center practitioners have done much as I have done here—I asked if we could put the paper, the assignment sheets, and related materials aside and just talk. I asked him how he was doing in school, how the season was going for him, and how he was handling his classes. He began to open up as we spoke. He explained the grind of his practice schedule, the strain he was experiencing in the long-distance relationship with his girlfriend from home, and his general discomfort in college. I could see the indifferent facade he attempted to maintain begin to relax, showing just how tired and worried he was.

We talked about some options to manage it all, and as we did so I took notes on what he said. We came back around to the subject of the paper—another source of stress for him—and I showed him the notes I had taken about our conversation. In short, he had a great deal he could write about in terms of identifying a problem and potential solutions. We talked about that, and I continued to make notes about some of what he was describing. We began brainstorming some directions he could take, and by the end of the session he was enthusiastic about the paper. He thanked me for helping him feel like he could handle it.

In the practicum meetings that followed, the class discussed the importance of setting the paper aside and working with the *person* rather than just the *writer*, of establishing rapport. After that semester, that tutor transferred to a college closer to home. I went on to use that example—anonymizing the tutor—in practicum courses afterward to emphasize the importance of rapport and the dangers in too quickly labeling writers as resistant. For that reason I stopped assigning the chapter of the *Bedford Guide* (2016) that deploys the phrase. I felt it gave tutors something of an alibi, language to easily categorize students and thus exempt themselves from the obligation of working with those students. I found it also tended to essentialize these writers into broad "types": the resistant writer, the writer who plagiarizes, the writer who comes in at the last moment, and so on.

That encounter gave me a concrete way to explain the dangers of these labels to my tutors, and for a while I felt good about using it. But something still bothered me about the narrative—beyond my own hubris and pride at accomplishing something one of my new and struggling tutors could not. For those years, however, I couldn't quite articulate what. I *knew* that essentializing writers as resistant was counterproductive. I *knew* that establishing rapport was important. I also knew that grounding these principles in actual examples of practice was important for new tutors. I also tried to be careful in how I shared these examples with tutors so that they wouldn't feel judged in their own practices. But still something wasn't quite right.

Of course, I began to recognize my own naivete and privilege in those early encounters, having neglected the gender and power dynamics in play in these encounters and, more importantly, my privilege as a white male professor in them. My subject position and authority provided an ethos that likely made the writer more responsive to my efforts. The tutor probably felt uncomfortable directly addressing power and gender dynamics (and their emotional toll) in a classroom with male students conducted by a male professor. She may have seen such an admission as a form of weakness or still another avenue in which to be dismissed. In short, by focusing on the affects of an individual or individual exchange, I failed to see how larger forces were acting on her sessions and her relationship with this writer.

But more than that, I came to realize that what had bothered me about the encounter was the implicit expectations and underlying assumptions about the exchange of affects—Arlie Hochschild's (2012) feeling rules—in the session and in the classroom. As Hochschild (2012) explained, "Acts of emotion management are not simply private acts; they are used in exchanges under the guidance of feeling rules. Feeling rules are standards used in emotional conversation to determine what is rightly owed and owing in the currency of feeling. Through them, we tell what is 'due' in each relation, each role" (p. 18).

I suppose that the tutor expected that writer to be less resistant because she had performed what she felt was the proper affect. She followed the feeling rules; that is, she mostly followed the directions in the *Bedford Guide* (2016): She was pleasant and courteous, greeted the writer cheerfully, asked questions, and more. In return, she expected a writer who, like in her other sessions, would incorporate her feedback, respond actively to her questions, and generally participate in the session. These affective displays would, for her, demonstrate a successful session. I wonder if she felt her "due" was some form of compliance. When the student did not comply with what she felt was the proper affect, it occasioned some emotional distress for her and called into question the value of her emotional labor. She was frustrated in the sessions and in the class. And though she was able to mask that frustration in the sessions, she shared it openly with us in the course.

And I suppose I expected that tutor to be more compliant because I performed what I felt was the proper affect for my role as her teacher. I wrote fully and sincerely in my responses to her practicum journal entries. I listened to her attentively in class discussions and validated her perceptions, paraphrased her, and offered suggestions grounded in the book we were all reading. I also wrote fully and sincerely in my responses to her formal writing assignments to offer suggestions for revisions when she resubmitted. In each of these endeavors, my response—my bodily feeling—to her resistance echoed her response to the baseball player's: I was frustrated with her, though I masked that feeling in class while I attempted to mentor her.

Each of us—the baseball player, the tutor, and I—were positioned affectively in those exchanges by our positioning in the university, by the circumstances acting upon us in those moments, and the roles we were expected to embody in those circumstances. Hochschild (2012) explained, "Taken together, emotion work, feeling rules, and interpersonal exchange make up our private emotional system. We bow to each other not only from the waist but from the heart. Feeling rules set out what is owed in gestures of exchange between people" (p. 76). These feeling rules, then, are not solely about how we bow to each other in discrete exchanges but rather connected to a network of exchanges and feeling rules. And teaching and tutoring are not a matter of simply facilitating learning but rather a matter of managing the emotion work necessary to facilitate learning, and this emotion work is itself informed by all of the other exchanges around it—between director and tutor, tutor and student, student and coach, student and girlfriend, student and other professors, tutor and other tutors, and so on.

And feeling rules extend still further: Teachers' affective labor works to encourage a change in the affects of students, making them more receptive to the discourse that instructor is teaching—which may, in turn, change those students' very subjectivity. In turn, students perform the perceived affects desired of them by their professors—demonstrating what is "due" per Hochschild's (2012) feeling rules—as enacted in class participation, in writing, or in exam performances. Put another way, these exchanges of affect are rhetorical, but they are also embodied and—as I will explain throughout this book—*felt*. The emotions of these exchanges circulate, and given their unique relationship to the university, the writing center is an interesting nodal point in this circulation. Emotional labor never occurs in isolation; rather, as Sara Ahmed (2004) has explained, "emotions work as a form of capital: affect does not reside positively in the sign or commodity, but is produced only as an effect of its circulation" (p. 120). That is, instead of residing solely as a psychic or individual phenomenon, emotions and affects move across situations, are commodified, and produce value. Emotional labor facilitates these exchanges; it, too, has value. As I hope my anecdote about the exchanges between me, my tutor, and the student illustrates, the emotional labor of the writing center session is located in larger economies (or perhaps ecologies) of affect.

Perhaps what distinguishes writing centers from other subfields or areas of rhetoric and writing studies is their unique situation as workplaces of students for student use. That is, they are pedagogical, they are peer-centered, they involve students taking courses across the disciplines, but they are also *jobs*. For all the term's popularization (and, according to its creator, possible overuse), *emotional labor* is perhaps the most powerful way of understanding how emotion and affect function in the writing center. This matters because the way emotions circulate in, say, the composition classroom is very different than in one-to-one interactions.

The nature of emotional labor in the center has also changed dramatically in the last few decades with the corporatization of the university. Several scholars have written about the causes and effects of the neoliberal "evolution" in universities such as Benjamin Ginsberg's (2011) *The Fall of the Faculty: The Rise of the All-Administrative University and Why it Matters* or Larry C. Gerber's (2014) *The Rise and Decline of Faculty Governance: Professionalization and the Modern American University*. But to put a fine point on it, adjusted for inflation, tuition rates have more than doubled since 1985 (NCES, n.d.) while faculty wages have remained relatively consistent. These trends mirror what the Economic Policy Institute has learned about the productivity-pay gap, wherein

> from 1979 to 2018, net productivity rose 69.6 percent, while the hourly pay of typical workers essentially stagnated—increasing only 11.6 percent over 39 years (after adjusting for inflation). This means that although Americans are working more productively than ever, the fruits of their labors have primarily accrued to those at the top and to corporate profits, especially in recent years. (EPI, 2026)

We are working harder than ever and being increasingly alienated from the products of that labor. And the price of one of the more potent tools for social class advancement—college—has far outpaced Americans' ability to pay for it.

The increased cost of tuition has clearly affected students too, making the stakes and fallout of their education higher than ever. And in this context, writing is often used as a measure in the larger gatekeeping and economic projects of the university: writing proficiency exams, standardized testing, final papers, and so on. The exorbitant costs of college alongside the economic incentives of completing a college degree mean that writing has become an ever more crucial component on students' "return on investment" and for "accountability" measures imposed on schools. Consequently, the work that occurs in writing center sessions is more than a simple conversation about writing. The stakes have material and often *life-altering* effects. Students naturally carry this context into the writing center with them.

This in turn has affected the sorts of labor performed at the writing center. Students are more desperate than ever to distinguish themselves from their peers once they're "on the market," and employment at the writing center is often one of those ways. And though writing tutor wages aren't usually more than the institution's minimum wage, tutors often rely on those wages. And that wage has stagnated relative to inflation over the last 20 years. Balancing studies, employment, and the other extracurricular and personal activities in this high-stakes context means that tutors are increasingly burned out, frazzled, distracted. They work with students who are experiencing much the same. In turn, these feelings often affect other employees at the center, who then must navigate that part of their emotional labor. Like students (and writing center administrators), tutors have never worked harder even as they are increasingly alienated from the products of their labor. And in these contexts, this labor frequently calls on writing center professionals to compromise in ways that may conflict with the grand narratives of home and coziness that McKinney (2012) has attributed to writing centers.

The goal of this book, then, is to grapple with the following questions: How do we account for, train for, and theorize emotion and affect in the writing center to facilitate better, more ethical practice? How might we ameliorate some of what Hochschild (2012) has described as the cost of emotional labor? How do we advocate for more just conditions in administering and managing emotional labor in these exchanges? Perhaps even more fundamentally I ask, *what does emotional labor in the writing center actually look like?*

The title of the book is a play on the title of the foundational book on threshold concepts in writing studies, *Naming What We Know* (Adler-Kassner & Wardle, 2015) and a *Composition Studies* article titled "Naming What We Feel: Hierarchical Microaggressions and the Relationship Between Composition and English Studies" (Brewer & di Gennaro, 2018). As Brewer and di Gennaro (2018) explained, their project

> has enabled [them] to "name what we feel," to borrow from the title of Linda Adler-Kassner and Elizabeth Wardle's book and the feminist political practice of naming, in which women share experiences and find ways to articulate common experiences previously assumed to be individual or personal. (30)

Similarly, my project here seeks to consider how we can learn to listen to what our bodies have to tell us. Rather than simply labeling *what* we feel, I am more interested here in learning *how* we feel and foster feeling. I am interested in feeling as a way of knowing and of facilitating (and being facilitated by) rhetoric.

Integral, then, to my arguments throughout this book is the notion that peer tutoring is an embodied genre—a discursive form responding to a recurring rhetorical situation—that needs to be analyzed in terms of its generic features to be more fully understood. Our feelings and our bodies are crucial—if often overlooked—features of that embodied genre. Identifying and articulating the work of those features is crucial to understanding not only our practice but the rich nature of emotional labor as it occurs. In turn, we may be able to abstract affective elements of the microcosm of the writing center session to begin theorizing about the rhetorical work of feeling around writing, discussions of and about writing, and the teaching of writing with more nuance and detail. In her own examination of representations of emotional labor in tutor training manuals, Bethany Mannon (2021) has suggested, "Future research might use interviews, observations, and surveys to study tutors' emotional labor during appointments" (p. 148). This monograph seeks to address and extend this call.

Emotional Labor Versus Emotion Work in Writing Center Studies

The turn to emotional labor in writing center studies is reflective of broader considerations of emotion and affect in composition studies (Benesch, 2012; Chandler, 2007; Lindquist, 2004; Micciche, 2007; Richmond, 2002; Robillard, 2007; Stenberg, 2011), in writing program administration (Adler-Kasner, 2008; Cole & Hassel, 2017; Davies, 2017; Holt et al., 2003; Micciche, 2002; Ritter, 2011; Sura et al., 2009; Wooten et al., 2020), and of course in writing centers (Driscoll & Wells, 2020; Giaimo, 2024; Jackson et al., 2016; Lape, 2008; Lawson, 2015; Perry, 2016).

Regarding writing centers, emotional labor has largely been explored in terms of its relationality and feeling. For example, Caswell et al. (2016) characterized emotional labor as an "invisible, but necessary element in person-to-person transactions" (p. 12). They further defined such labors as "those tasks a director completed or contemplated when the task involved nurturing, encouraging, and building relationships or resolving conflicts" (Caswell et al., 2016, pp. 25–26). Caswell et al. thus focus on the relational dimensions of the director position. Much of the subsequent work on emotional labor in writing center contexts is similarly oriented. Many of the essays in *Out in the Center*, for instance, focus on the relationship between intersectionality, identity, and emotional labor. For example, Richard Sévère (2019) explained that "specifically, the perceived threat of the black male body (in media) has implored me to search for other bodies of color (directors and otherwise) in writing center work—a search for guidance, mentorship, comfort, empathy and support" (p. 43). Relational configurations of emotional labor appear elsewhere in that collection, such as in Anna Rita Napoleone's (2019) and Beth Towle's (2019) essays on affect and class in the writing center. Similarly, much of Travis Webster's (2021) monograph considers the relational work inherent in being an LGBTQIA director in hetero- and cisnormative spaces.

The relational dimensions of emotion work appear in other writing center contexts as well. Mattingly et al. (2021) discussed training online tutors in emotional intelligence, writing that "specifically, we focus on how a year-long EI training series enabled our team to identify the emotional challenges of writing center work and *how we could healthfully manage this labor through a culture of connectedness, empathy, and trust*" ("Cultivating," emphasis mine). Kate Navickas and various coauthors (2020, 2022) have considered more identity-oriented feeling work around "becoming" the role. Likewise, several of the essays in *Emotions and Affect in Writing Centers* (Morris & Concannon, 2022) rely on this more global, relational sense of the term. Chavannes et al. (2022), for instance, rely on Mara Holt et al.'s (2003) definition of emotional labor as "responsive attention to the emotional aspects of social life, including attention to personal feelings, the emotional tenor of relationships, empathy, and encouragement, mediation of disputes, building emotional solidarity in groups, and using one's own or other's *outlaw emotions* to interrogate structures" (p. 147). Finally, Kristi Murray Costello (2021) drew on several theorists of emotional labor (including Hochschild) to explain that "all work is emotional labor, but some forms of work demand emotional connections with others" (p. xi).

I emphasize writing center studies' focus on emotion and relationality in labor contexts to draw attention to what Hochschild—in an interview for *The Atlantic* (Beck, 2018)—herself has identified as the "concept creep" of the term. If "all work is emotional labor," it becomes nearly impossible to speak meaningfully about emotional labor and what distinguishes it from work that simply involves the emotions. This distinction is crucial, as Hochschild explained it, because it can lead to having "an important conversation . . . in a hazy way, working with a blunt concept" (Beck, 2018). Much of the work of this book is trying to be as specific as possible—to put names to emotional labor by identifying its components.

Emotional Labor, Concept Creep, Surface- and Deep-Acting

In that interview, Hochschild summarized her own view of emotional labor as

> the work, for which you're paid, which centrally involves trying to feel the right feeling for the job. This involves evoking and suppressing feelings. Some jobs require a lot of it, some a little of it. From the flight attendant whose job it is to be nicer than natural to the bill collector whose job it is to be, if necessary, harsher than natural, there are a variety of jobs that call for this. Teachers, nursing-home attendants, and child-care workers are examples. The point is that while you may also be doing physical labor and mental labor, you are crucially being hired and monitored for your capacity to manage and produce a feeling. (Beck, 2018)

When asked if sharing ideas in a meeting in a nonthreatening way qualifies as emotional labor, Hochschild responded, "Not unless it is experienced as anxiety-provoking or fear-evoking to you" (Beck, 2018). That is, work is only emotional labor if there is a discrepancy between the displayed affect and the feeling. Put still another way, not all work is emotional labor, and more critically, *not all relational work is emotional labor*. Sometimes the required countenance aligns with what we feel. While every writing center session is permeated with emotion and affect, and while relationality inflects everything we do in the center, it is not always emotional labor in its technical sense. And this technical sense matters because there is a wealth of empirical research from a variety of fields exploring emotional labor, and this research has a great deal to offer writing center studies.

According to management researchers Yun-Tsan and Yi-Chih (2017), "the concept of emotional labor was grounded on Goffman's [dramaturgical] theory" (p. 2). This theory "holds that people will disguise themselves or wear different masks like actors and show behavior specific to that role so as to give or maintain a good impression in front of others" (Yun-Tsan & Yi-Chih, 2017, p. 2). In brief, though originally conceived in the workplace, emotional labor more broadly refers to the work necessary to take on the affective and emotional display rules required of a particular situation or set of circumstances (Grandey, 2000; Hochschild, 2012; Kruml & Geddes, 2000; Lee & Ok, 2012; Mesmer-Magnus et al., 2012). Hochschild (2012) explained that employees have two means by which to do this work: change their outward displays to match expectations (surface acting) or change their actual feelings to be more consistent with these expectations (deep acting). Researchers such as Grandey (2000) as well as Kruml and Geddes (2000) have since translated Hochschild's (2012) original concepts of surface and deep acting into two interrelated dimensions of emotional labor: emotional dissonance (ED) and emotional effort (EE).

Conceptually, emotional dissonance and surface acting have been used interchangeably (Morris & Feldman, 1996; Zapf, 2002), though there are subtle distinctions worth noting. As described by Lee and Ok (2012), emotional dissonance "occurs when employees fake, suppress, or amplify emotional expressions that differ from their true feelings" (p. 1102). As Lee and Ok (2012) have explained, "Surface acting implies a state of ED because almost any employee in a job involving manipulating emotions will experience ED to some extent" (1102). When one's true feelings are at odds with the requirements of the role and situation, one is in a state of dissonance. When someone in this state adopts an external affect to match the situation, that person is surface acting.

By contrast, emotional effort and deep acting refer to when a person actively tries to change their feelings or emotional state to more clearly align with the expectations of the role (Grandey, 2000; Kruml & Geddes, 2000). Whereas surface acting emphasizes matching external displays of affect in line with expectations while retaining one's true emotions (hence emotional dissonance), deep acting instead internalizes those expectations (which, in turn, requires emotional effort). Deep acting is labor in that a person works to change how they feel.

In this book, I rely on Hochschild's (2012) description of emotional labor as requiring "one to induce or suppress feeling in order to sustain the outward countenance that produces the proper state of mind in others—in this case, the sense of being cared for in a convivial and safe place" (p. 7). Here I differ from many other writing center scholars' use of Hochschild (2012) in that I locate emotional labor most specifically in surface- and deep-acting behaviors—in what it takes to sustain the outward countenance. I believe the emphasis on outward countenance is a crucial distinction from more common conceptions of emotion work in writing centers for two reasons. First, such a conception locates emotional labor in the body, and second, it focuses on the production of a "proper state of mind in others," highlighting the rhetorical nature of emotional labor.

I don't deny the importance of studying the more global, relational dimensions of emotional labor in the writing center; if anything, such work indicates the need for considering the particulars of surface acting and deep acting, of what we mean when we induce or suppress feeling, and of the cost of caring. Hochschild's (2012) emphasis on the dissonance between what is felt and what the rhetorical situation calls for is also crucial in that it encourages us to be more specific with our terms—distinguishing, for example, between emotion, affect, and feeling—in ways that can be generative.

Though the terms *emotion* and *affect* can be used interchangeably in most contexts, I do wish to take a moment to distinguish between the two. For Napoleone (2019), "emotion is understood as an experience that can be defined, coherent, and understood; whereas, affect 'is something that is *before* emotions' and is seen as a bodily reaction or a direct response that is prior to consciousness" (Åhäll, qtd. in Napoleone, 2019, p. 84). However, like Ahmed, Napoleone acknowledges that though there can be a distinction, they are not necessarily separate. And for my purposes in this book, although affect could be understood as occurring before emotions, affect is also an embodied act that displays emotions—affect *emotes*.

Michael Hardt and Antonio Negri (2005), for instance, distinguished affect from emotions,

> which are mental phenomena, affects refer equally to body and mind. In fact, affects, such as joy and sadness, reveal the present state of life in the entire organism, expressing a certain state of the body along with a certain mode of thinking. (p. 108)

In short, emotions are internal phenomena, whereas affects imply physical, material phenomena. Affects are observable, and even measurable. Though I'll speak to the distinction later, for my purposes here, affects are useful for practitioners because they can signal and engender visible changes in the affect of others. In short, affect—outward display—is the means through which emotional labor occurs.

Hochschild (2012) further explicated the relationship between feeling, emotion, and affect when she defined emotional labor as the "management of feeling to create a publicly observable facial and bodily display" (p. 7). For her, feeling is a process of discovery, defining feeling,

> like emotion, as a sense, like the sense of hearing or sight. In a general way, we experience it when bodily sensations are joined with what we see or imagine. Like the sense of hearing, emotion communicates information. It has, as Freud said of anxiety, a "signal function." From feeling we discover our own viewpoint on the world. (Hochschild, 2012, p. 17)

Her emphasis on signal functions and discovery is crucial for rhetoricians to consider in that it echoes Doug Downs's (2020) discussion of rhetoric beginning in bodies, of rhetoric as signal intelligence, "because rhetoric is ultimately about the ways that we make sense of and respond to the many signals in our experience of the moment—signals from other people, from our surroundings, and from our own bodies" (p. 463). Feelings are signals from the body, coconstructed with other signals from the world and other senses, and they are negotiated as part of larger processes of meaning-making. In short, the body is a cocontributor in the rhetoric and emotional labor of the writing center session.

But feelings are not isolated signals sent from the body to the mind. Rather, as Hochschild (2012) has explained, feelings are negotiated, regulated, and—with deep acting (or emotional effort)—changed to fit the needs of the situation. Accordingly, throughout the book I emphasize identifying *how* we feel rather than simply naming *what* we may feel. Micciche (2007) asserted that "emotions do something besides express individuals' feelings . . . emotions function as the adhesive that aligns certain bodies together and binds a person/position/role to an affective state" (p. 75). If we wish to better understand how bodies and feelings engage with labor—how we align bodies and roles to affective states—I argue throughout this book that we need a common lexicon to name and theorize them. Chapters 1 and 2 especially focus on what the specific affect coding system (SPAFF) has to offer writing center practitioners for naming our feelings and how they relate to our practice. Focusing on the *how* of feelings emphasizes the agential and rhetorical importance of emotional labor: how we read and compose bodies.

Tutoring as Embodied Genre

The idea of bodily literacy is not new to those studying embodied rhetoric. Kristie Fleckenstein (2003), for example, asserted that "a corporeal literacy points us to the material dimension of writing-reading, to meaning's reliance on our physical participation in the world" (p. 46). That is, writing and reading are not simply mental acts occurring apart from bodies; rather, they are physical acts that occur through and with bodies. Garrett et al. (2012) extended Fleckenstein's claims to the act of invention itself—usually seen solely as a mental activity, observing that "attention to the physical body in invention practices, as a centralized piece of the meaning-making process, makes explicit the minute, involuntary, and habitual ways in which individual bodies make contact with other bodies, other texts, other external objects/subjects in the world" (Scene 2, para. 2). Even terms typically associated with the canons of rhetoric such as, say, invention (e.g., brainstorming) or revision (re-seeing) invoke the body: brains and eyes. In any act of writing, then, the body is always already inextricably imbricated as a medium and as a bodily rhetor. The body thus communicates through feeling, and we can learn to listen.

That, very briefly, is the basic notion of embodied rhetoric: that the body is a modality and rhetor in the conveyance of meaning. As a field of study, embodied rhetoric incorporates elements from ethnography, postcolonialism, feminism, and other methodologies and theoretical perspectives that emphasize how positionality shapes the production and expression of knowledge. And I want to be very clear here that I'm not equating a rhetorical body with an author—as we all know, particularly in American society, some bodies are authorized more than others. Sévère (2019), for example, points out the trouble of assuming such in the use of his body as a messenger when he says,

> Though I hope that message is positive and dynamic in nature, and I realize that in many instances it is depending on the context and who is receiving the message, there are moments in which my six-foot-two-inch-two-hundred-pound frame is engaging others in a negative dialogue unbeknownst to my consciousness. (p. 45)

Rather, I want to stress the body as a nexus in the circulation of rhetoric—a space wherein various discourses converge and are contested.

And though writing center studies has explored genres and examined how tutors and writers work with them in the writing center, we don't necessarily consider what genre studies has to offer us in terms of the physical, embodied act of facilitating a writing center session as a genre itself. I assert that our pedagogy is indeed a patterned genre and that like any patterned genre, writing tutoring occurs with and through bodies and is contextually bound. If genres, as defined by Carolyn Miller (1984), are "typified rhetorical actions based in recurrent situations," (p. 159), then writing center sessions are clearly a genre. In Bakhtinian terms, the session is a secondary genre intended to facilitate an intervention in and possible reconsideration of a writer's work, inflected differently than that of, say, the teacher conference, or an editor's intervention. In turn, the consultant draws on several primary speech genres such as those described by Summer Smith (1997) in her work on the genre of teacher end comments. These speech genres, for instance, include judging genres, reader response genres, and coaching genres (Smith, 1997, pp. 252–261). These genres, of course, are inflected by their modalities: the way one raises or lowers one's voice, the proximity with which they sit next to their conversation partner, the manner of dress, facial expressions, and so on, are all generic features that facilitate the rhetorical action of the session. As such, when considering the body as a multimodal site for meaning-making, it behooves us to consider its role as a feature in the genre of the writing center session.

At the same time, however, we must be mindful of Miller's (1984) caution that "a rhetorically sound definition of genre must be centered not on the substance or form of discourse but on the action it is used to accomplish" (p. 151). I worry, for instance, that in the advice from guidebooks on embodied representations in the writing center, such as when Ryan and Zimmerelli (2016) have urged consultants to "sit in a relaxed and comfortable manner, and demonstrate interest in the writer's words by leaning forward and making eye contact," (p. 12) we focus on the form rather than the action it is used to accomplish. Such formulations may also unwittingly convey ableist or ethnocentric assumptions about what bodies expect of other bodies.

For example, such a seated posture—leaning close and maintaining eye contact—may communicate welcome, receptivity, and familiarity to some bodies, but it may also communicate scrutiny, suspicion, or contempt to other bodies. The bodies, of course, may include the variety of neurodiverse writers who come to the center. The concerns I raise here for tutors might also be said for whatever inferences we draw from observing sessions as researchers.

What I argue throughout the book, then, is that we need a common tongue to more accurately describe and theorize affects and emotional labor, rather than taking a prescriptive approach—such as leaning forward and making eye contact—to the body in the session. I wish for us to adopt a more genre-oriented understanding. Most of all, I want us to work toward understanding the body and emotions as *modalities* that figure in the genre of the peer tutoring session. Crucial to this understanding is that if the peer tutoring session is a genre, and the body and affects are features of the genre, we need to interrogate the genre from a critical, intersectional perspective to ask, who is authorized to use this genre, who benefits from it, who is excluded, and how does power circulate within it? As Napoleone (2019) has observed, emotions in the center are regulated and inexorably bound to identity performance. A critical genre pedagogy applied to writing center sessions thus asks us to be more mindful of who is served by emotional labor. Naming what—and how—we feel is an important step toward facilitating this mindfulness.

Chapter Breakdown

I have organized the following chapters to allow exploration and expansion of the practice of emotional labor in the writing center, beginning first with how we might identify it and understand it, then moving outward to how tutors experience it and its relationship to other concepts associated with emotion such as emotional intelligence and burnout, before considering how we might train tutors for affect and emotional labor. I conclude by considering how we might advocate for more equitable conditions for emotional labor within our writing centers by engaging with our institutions. Put another way, I start small—within the session—and expand outward to trace the ways in which affect circulates within the session, among the staff, within the center more broadly, and within the institution.

This book compiles case studies considering emotional labor from different angles. And while emotional labor permeates the writing center, this book does not attempt to comprehensively address it in its whole. Rather, it explores a series of case studies and posits them as fairly emblematic of various dimensions of emotional labor in the American writing center. In essence, this book is the story—and tells stories—of efforts to better understand and account for emotion in my own center. My hope is that these stories will provide researchers and directors resources to do the same in their centers. As such, I open many chapters with a narrative to ground the exigence of the chapter's questions or to illustrate the implications for the chapter's arguments. Throughout the book I share coding schema and training documents, and I detail the assorted methods I've undertaken for some of the case studies I present.

In Chapter 1, I explain the specific affect coding system (the SPAFF) and our staff's efforts to adapt it to writing center contexts. The SPAFF is a framework designed by psychologists to identify and analyze discrete instances of affective display. Although originally developed by Coan and Gottman (2007) to observe affect in marital and counseling situations, the SPAFF has been adapted for other contexts. In this chapter, I share a summary of the SPAFF and explain the process by which we adapted it for writing center contexts. I share descriptions of each code and how to apply it, and I share some protocols for how it might be used in the writing center for different purposes. If emotional labor occurs when a preferred display countenance is at odds with one's actual feelings, the SPAFF can provide a means by which to identify elements of that countenance. This adaptation and application of the SPAFF to a new domain seeks to demonstrate its potential utility and contribute to the understanding of affective display in a new context. I also apply the modified SPAFF to a case study of a session to consider its implications.

Chapter 2 is composed of two further case studies, pairing the SPAFF with codes examining collaboration and control to consider the emotional labor of two new writing center consultants. It examines those consultants' attempts to translate their training into actual practice, focusing especially on how new consultants navigate issues of authority in sessions and how they use affect to facilitate those negotiations. This chapter seeks to share examples of how researchers can apply our adaptation of the SPAFF and to highlight the role of emotional labor as it relates to certain commonplaces in writing center practice.

To get at what Hochschild (2012) wonders about "the human cost of becoming an 'instrument of labor' at all" (p. 3), I consider the toll of emotional labor in the writing center in Chapter 3. Hochschild (2012) observed that "beneath the difference between physical and emotional labor, there lies a similarity in the possible cost of doing the work: the worker can become estranged or alienated from an aspect of self—either the body or the margins of the soul—that is *used* to do the work" (p. 7). In brief, the unique character of emotional labor thus implies an alienation from a different sort of means of production than manual labor: that of the emotions themselves. Chapter 3 studies this phenomenon, sharing the results of focus group interviews with tutors to better understand how they articulate the cost of emotional labor in the writing center. I find that while the tutors interviewed found satisfaction in their work and overall did not find it to be stressful, guilt and cynicism were two powerful concepts that arose in the interviews, warranting further examination.

Emotional intelligence (EI) is a key concept emerging in the data of Chapters 2 and 3, and as such is explored more fully in Chapter 4. Emotional intelligence can play a crucial role in managing and performing emotional labor effectively. It is the ability to recognize, understand, and manage one's own emotions and effectively perceive and respond to the emotions of others. It encompasses skills such as self-awareness, self-regulation, empathy, and social skills. Studies such as Lee & Ok's (2012) examination of workers in the hospitality industry have demonstrated how employees' EI influences the sorts of emotional effort (or deep acting) and emotional dissonance (surface acting) they perform, and how EI mediates burnout and job satisfaction in emotional labor. But there is another dimension of emotional intelligence: what some researchers have referred to as its "dark side." In brief, "emotionally intelligent people may manipulate others' behaviors to suit their own interests using high-level capabilities to read and manage the emotions of others" (Nozaki & Koyasu, 2013, p. 1). Chapter 4 thus asks us to reconsider emotional intelligence and asks us to train tutors for it in more intersectional, mindful ways. I argue in this chapter that we need to conceive of the peer tutoring session as a genre, and that critical genre pedagogy into tutor training—training for the genre of the session—writing center directors can foster a more inclusive and equitable environment.

I conclude the book by focusing on the *labor* part of "emotional labor," locating it in a larger system of affective exchange embedded in the university system. If we wish to enact more just and balanced approaches to emotional labor in the writing center, I argue that we need to contextualize our work in the larger affective projects of our institutions.

Looking Backward and Forward: Naming Emotion

In considering the exchanges between the baseball player, my tutor, and me, I now see the ways in which we each emotionally labored. For my part, I was laboring to enact what I thought to be the preferred display affect required of my role as a professor. My own working-class, first-generation background had long caused me to doubt my ability to "pass" as a "real academic." I think in trying to maintain my academic distance—especially as a new professor—I neglected opportunities for care with the tutor. I think, for instance, I could have acknowledged and perhaps exceeded the "feeling rules" that informed these exchanges. I believe I could have kindly shared my concerns with her performance in the class and been more direct about why I suspect she struggled with the student. At the same time, I think I could have taken her frustrations into consideration more, recognizing that the unspoken gender dynamics at play likely influenced the session. I wonder if I could have spoken more with the baseball player to get a sense of his perspective on the relationship between him and his tutor. I wonder about the conditions that we all were laboring under. Ironically, I was so concerned for professionalism, for impartiality, that I lost sight of the actual people embodying these roles, even as I was encouraging my tutors to work with the *person* as much as the *writer*—a facile distinction if ever there were one. I believe that had I known more about the very idea of "feeling rules," of affect, and what we expect of it, we could each have had more generative, meaningful exchanges.

Mannon (2021) demonstrated that many of our field's discussions of emotion and training materials don't often refer to emotion and emotion management as skills to practice; rather there is often an underlying assumption that those skills are innate. She explained, "Some tutors may indeed have those qualities when beginning the job. However, treating emotional labor as natural, easy, or 'not real work' (Hochschild, 2009, 2013, p. 30) leads to a writing center where the work of managing writers' emotions is invisible, devalued, and disheartening" (Mannon, 2021, p. 145). I believe that, despite studying emotion and affect at that time, I had assumed the same. Worse, that tutor's emotional labor was rendered invisible and thus unvalued because of my inability to consider it, enacting Arlene Kaplan Daniels's (1987) observation about the gendered nature of invisible work.

My hope is that efforts such as these will help render this invisible labor knowable and nameable. And so named, I hope we can begin to understand it in such a way that improves not only our practice, but the health of the communities in which that practice is embedded. Such work, as Giaimo (2023) has pointed out, is not only theoretical and scholarly, not only material and affective, but political as well, being "intimately tied to our identities and relative positionality within the broader institution" (p. 16). To advocate for conditions of equitable emotional labor within our centers is to advocate more broadly. With this project I hope to offer tutors, directors, and researchers a language with which to describe both the emotions they feel and those they seek to convey. I hope this language will help them understand why they feel those emotions and why they are seeking to convey particular emotions at particular times. I hope it will provide writing center administrators training tools to help tutors be more mindful in this process. I hope that it will provide researchers with codes and methods to explore the circulation of affect in a variety of contexts in and around writing centers. I hope it might provide writing across the curriculum coordinators and writing center administrators new ways to engage with faculty and other university stakeholders. I hope it will prompt us to ask to what end emotional labor is being deployed, and for whose benefit. I hope it is for more than mere compliance.

In the end, however, I mostly hope it will simply contribute to furthering empathy and good practice.

1

Developing Specific Affect Codes for Writing Center Contexts

Years ago, I set about trying to understand the role of affect and emotion in the writing center session. Though researchers have worked to unpack the genre of the writing center session through looking at motivational scaffolding and politeness (Mackiewicz & Thompson, 2013), tutor questioning strategies (Mackiewicz & Thompson, 2018), tutor collaborative moves (Harris, 1986), collaboration and ethics (Clark, 1988), and more, there still hasn't been a thorough breakdown of emotions in that genre. Spurred on by Babcock and Thonus's (2012) observation that there was little replicable, aggregable, and data-driven (RAD) research in that area, I looked around for ways to describe what I was seeing in a way that others could replicate. As I began recording sessions to engage in some ethnographic observation, I wanted some way to move beyond an impressionistic sense of the affective displays I was seeing. I wanted some way to point to discrete behaviors and know with some reliability that I was observing a particular emotion. I wanted some way to "denaturalize" the seemingly obvious work of emotion in sessions, some way to take what seems normal and break it down into its parts without reducing it to those things. Although I saw the value in more open approaches to coding, I understood that other fields had likely developed systematized ways of looking at affect that could be borrowed for the writing center.

https://doi.org/10.7330/9781646428649.c001

In that search, I found the specific affect coding system (SPAFF), an instrument developed by psychologists to code for displays of affect between married couples and later adapted for other situations. Its use has since been expanded for other situations including support groups (Giese-Davis et al., 2005), team performance and intragroup conflict (Jung, 2016), as well as "interactions among children, their parents, and their peers . . . and even to therapy situations" (Coan & Gottman, 2007, p. 267). Researchers have thus adapted the SPAFF for coding a variety of affective interactions beyond its origins in marital counseling. I have used it previously in a *WLN: A Journal of Writing Center Scholarship* article (Lawson, 2015) to categorize how various writing center scholars described emotion, and Mannon (2021) has used it to examine how emotional labor has been described in tutor training manuals, finding that it "makes possible a more precise discussion of emotion and emotional labor than previous writing center scholarship has achieved" (p. 150).

Early in my research, an assistant and I were able to apply the codes fairly predictably as we tested the instrument. However, as I revisited the sessions, I became less worried about reliability and more with validity. That is, I was concerned that what we were seeing was not necessarily a genuine reflection of how tutors comported themselves during sessions. Rather, I worried that the presence of the camera (and the accompanying IRB consent forms) had affected their performance, enacting the observer's paradox or Hawthorne effect—that they were performing for me as their boss rather than performing for and with their session partner. So I started to realize that the SPAFF likely functions differently in these sorts of contexts than in romantic and personal relationships.

As I learned more about emotional labor, it also affected how *I* understood the sessions and those performances. Even if what I was examining wasn't necessarily representative of their practice in general, it was still very revealing in displaying what tutors understood to be the proper display affect for their roles. Though I may not have been seeing a generalizable snapshot into their use of affect in sessions, I was seeing how they thought *I* wanted to see them perform. I thus became less interested in what might generally happen during a session and more in what tutors believed should happen—what Hochschild (2012) described as the "outward countenance" they were laboring to achieve. I was seeing their emotional labor.

At the same time, I began to better understand the limitations of the instrument I was using and the limitations my own context was imposing on my use of the instrument. Many of the indicators of the SPAFF were still rooted in its marriage counseling contexts. While it has been adopted to other contexts, it hadn't been done for the writing center. More crucially, however, the SPAFF typically requires months of intensive training to apply as well as a significant financial investment in outsourcing the training. This may be standard for research centers embedded in R1 psychology and counseling departments, but most writing centers don't have access to these sorts of resources. If I wanted to develop a tool for writing center researchers to study affect in writing center contexts that could also serve as a tool for training writing center tutors for affect and emotional labor, I realized that such a tool needed to be responsive to those contexts and constraints.

Consequently, in the spring of 2023, I recruited several writing center consultants to study, apply, and revise the SPAFF for our writing center. We took them off the regular schedule each week for an hour. A week or so ahead of our first meeting, I shared Coan and Goffman's article detailing the SPAFF so that they could fluently discuss it in that meeting. I also shared a video recording of a writing center session and a transcription (obtained with IRB approval). I explained that we would spend each meeting attempting to apply the SPAFF to the recorded session, discussing how we interpreted the codes and negotiating how we might revise the codes. Over the next several months in our research meetings, we would watch a few minutes of the video, review the transcript, and code. We would then discuss how we coded each snippet and why and discuss the weakness of the coding system as it was or what we saw in the video that felt like it should be coded but wasn't.

The following chapter describes the SPAFF and what it may have to offer writing center researchers and practitioners.

What Is the Specific Affect Coding System (SPAFF)?

The specific affect coding system (SPAFF) is a coding system that is both mutually exclusive and exhaustive, producing a continuous flow of behavioral data for every participant being coded. It was developed to observe affective behavior beyond extremely discrete bits of physical behaviors such as gestures or facial movements. Coan and Gottman (2007) divide affect codes into two categories outside of "neutral" states: positive and negative (Table 1.1).

As explained by Coan and Gottman (2007), the codes are latent psychological constructs that are not directly observable. Rather, as they describe it, the core, latent construct "is assumed to exist and to actually *cause* the expression of its various observable indicators" (Coan & Gottman, 2007, p. 268).

That is, someone experiencing an affect will behave in ways that enable others to observe it. Each code comes with a description of the construct's *function*, a list of *indicators, physical cues* associated with the construct, and a list of *counterindicators*. The function is an explanation of the code; the indicators are a list of behaviors typically associated with the affect; physical cues are nonverbal behaviors that can help observers identify the occurrence of the affect; and counterindicators are behaviors that can often be mistaken for indicators associated with the code but actually indicate a different affect (or none at all).

TABLE 1.1. Coan and Gottman (2007), Original Codes

Positive Affects	Negative Affects
· Affection	· Anger
· Enthusiasm	· Belligerence
· Humor	· Contempt
· Interest	· Criticism
· Validation	· Defensiveness
	· Disgust
	· Domineering
	· Fear/Tension
	· Sadness
	· Stonewalling
	· Threats
	· Whining

For example, someone feeling the construct "Validation" may display *indicators* such as agreeing or apologizing, summarizing or paraphrasing their partner's words, and/or nodding their head and maintaining eye contact. Someone affecting Validation may also demonstrate additional *physical cues* that can include "the Cheek Raiser and Lid Compressor" (AU 6) alongside "the Lip Corner Puller" (AU 12) (Coan & Gottman, 2007, p. 272). Finally, Validation has several *counterindicators* that may confuse coders at first. For instance, sentence-finishing is common in Validation, but if it's done in such a way as to interrupt a speaker or seize the conversational floor, this may actually be an instance of Domineering. Thus, each code provides counterindicators in anticipation of potential confusion.

In all, these behavioral indicators and counterindicators point to an underlying affect. As Coan and Gottman (2007) explained,

> it is of little specific consequence to us as SPAFF coders whether we observe direct statements of agreement or apology, whether we observe summarizing behaviors, or whether we observe head-nodding behavior with eye contact. These bits of observation are merely the media through which we become aware of the thing we are really interested in, which is Validation. We cannot "see" Validation without the presence of one or more or its indicators, but without the construct of Validation, those indicators are by themselves of little theoretical value. (p. 268)

The individual indicators are thus the medium through which the underlying affect communicates. This stance is one that is inherently rhetorical and thus one that is appropriate for writing center practitioners: once we understand the session as a social genre, we can see not only how we may communicate through emotion but how emotion communicates through us.

The rhetorical nature of the SPAFF also helps it stand out from other coding systems in that it is particularly context-bound. While this enhances the SPAFF's potency, it also requires a sort of cultural informant system where the categories and thresholds for emotion coding need to be adjusted to accurately reflect the research data's context. As Coan and Gottman (2007) described it,

> the cultural-informant approach utilizes individuals who are, for one reason or another, sensitive observers in a specific cultural setting. They may, for example, have specific knowledge about a certain culture or group of cultures and, by virtue of this specific knowledge, be uniquely capable of decoding the meaning of specific behaviors within the context of that culture. Anthropologists have employed cultural informants to study cultures with which they were not intuitively familiar. Cultural informants aid researchers in the interpretation of specific observable events. (p. 269)

The cultural informant approach is especially valuable to members of a community of practice such as the writing center. These insiders have specific knowledge of the community, so they can understand behavior in those contexts. Given the nature of such a coding system, however, it is crucial to ensure that the thresholds and emotions coded within a specific context are not simply transferred from a completely different context. Because writing center sessions do not generate the same heightened levels of affect observed in marital conflicts, we thus had to modify the instrument to more accurately capture that context.

The Changes We Made and Why We Made Them

While the SPAFF is useful for identifying discrete instances of emotion in social interactions, we had to make changes. The most obvious changes we had to make were bound up in the differences in context between using SPAFF to examine therapeutic and marriage counseling interactions versus educational situations. Although, as I have outlined in the Introduction, research has demonstrated the highly emotional and affective nature of writing center work, that work occurs in a professional setting and is thus far less intimate than, say, marital or counseling contexts. And while the valence of displayed emotion may tend to be of less magnitude than in those contexts, it is still present in writing center sessions and requires a form of labor to adjudicate. And as Mannon (2021) has observed, we often take fluency in this adjudication as a given in our tutors. Accordingly, my staff and I collaborated to revise the codes to address that context more accurately. We also had to reckon with the limitations not only of the context of the writing center session but of writing centers' resources in general.

Time, for example, was a significant factor in our decision to adapt the codes. On the one hand, as Giese-Davis et al. (2005) explained, the SPAFF—as opposed to other coding systems—is relatively time-efficient: "Many coding systems require a few hours of coding for just a few minutes of video. SPAFF coding typically takes about one to three times the number of minutes of video" (p. 403). However, professional training for the SPAFF can take weeks or months. Such training is also expensive. While these expenses can be borne by a funded research lab, writing centers typically do not have these sorts of resources available to them. This cost would be further prohibitive if we wish to use coding systems like the SPAFF to help tutors become more fluent in emotion and outward display.

In adapting the SPAFF codes, we had two purposes: first, to conduct research on affect and emotional labor in writing center contexts, and second, to provide tutors with a usable framework for developing their own emotional intelligence (in writing center contexts) through monitoring their partners' and their own emotional states. We thus had to make the codes accessible to laypersons. In service to this task, we made several alterations as we rewrote the SPAFF. First, we collapsed some codes—putting them together—to make them more accessible. For example, most of our team of coders found—particularly regarding many of the "negative" affects—that those affects didn't occur frequently enough in writing center sessions to warrant the distinction between similar categories. In the original SPAFF (Coan & Gottman, 2007), for instance, Belligerence and Contempt are distinct and important enough categories to be divided. Contempt especially is important in the context of marital conflict and counseling as its presence tends to be one of the best indicators of divorce, whereas Belligerence is not. That said, for writing center purposes, those categories were close enough that we felt it easiest to simply conflate and overlap them. We had similar thoughts about the codes Domineering and Threats, treating Threats as a magnitude of Domineering behavior. Given that the SPAFF already describes Threats as "a particularly hostile form of domineering behavior" (Coan & Gottman, 2007, p. 280), we felt it simpler and more accessible for tutors to put them together. We also did this with some of the indicators within codes, finding that our coders often got distracted by trying to identify which indicator of a code a particular instance of behavior was rather than simply acknowledging that the indicator alerted us to the underlying affect all the same. Some indicators—inappropriate for the writing center workplace context, such as the Reminiscing indicator of Affection—were removed altogether.

Similarly—and probably most substantively—we modified and authored language around the function or attributes of the latent construct (as well as Indicators) to be more specific to writing center workplace contexts. Most especially, we focused on providing examples of behaviors and utterances that would help tutors identify instances of that affect. For instance, in the SPAFF, Affection "expresses genuine caring and concern and offers comfort. Often the voice slows and becomes quieter or lower. Its function is to facilitate closeness and bonding" (Coan & Gottman, 2007, p. 272). While these qualities can certainly be present in a writing center session, we didn't want layperson tutors to be confused or distracted by phrasing such as "offers comfort," or "closeness and bonding." Consequently, although we kept some of this verbiage, we emphasized rapport, as this is not only a common goal in writing center sessions but also implicit in many of the indicators of Affection such as "common cause" and "empathy."

Although we kept most of the indicators of the SPAFF, we provided more writing center-specific instances for researchers and practitioners. For example, for the Caring Statements indicator of Affection, the SPAFF provides sentences such as "I love you" or "I care about you." We provided example alternative caring statements that would be appropriate displays of affection and care in the writing center such as "I want to make sure we're using your time well" or "I hope spring break is great!" We worked to provide sample utterances like these for each code to make them as accessible as possible for tutors being trained. As insiders in the culture of the center, tutors are especially attuned to the tropes and rhetorical nature of these utterances, and thus we found the sample statements to be especially powerful in terms of orienting those coders.

Finally, we attuned the codes to tutor identity, as Giaimo (2023) has observed that "emotional labor is [bound up] with class, race, gender, and other circumstances that are particular to individual workers" (p. 112). In our discussions about the codes and indicators, we extended this to culture, (dis)ability, and neurodiversity. Although the SPAFF has been adapted to international contexts (Banks, 2018) and has been examined in terms of race and bias (Babcock &

Banks, 2019), we were hesitant to apply SPAFF codes without grounding them in those vital bits of context.

Our Version of the SPAFF

The following codes are summary descriptions of the codes with brief examples of indicators. A fuller description of the codes (such as I used for the coding done in Chapter 2) can be found in Appendix A. I also include a handout like what follows in Appendix B.

Our SPAFF Protocol

Although I provide concrete examples of analysis done using this adaptation of the SPAFF in the next chapter, I share here the protocol our center adapted for its use. These can be adapted for research, for staff training, or for similar purposes.

1. **DETERMINE YOUR QUESTIONS OR PURPOSE.** What about display affect do I want to learn in this session or writing center scenario? Is this a research project or for training? Am I working to train a few tutors or several? Are we delving into one particular aspect of emotional labor or many? Knowing your question will help you bound the scope of the project.

2. **PRACTICE CODING.** The SPAFF is a context-dependent instrument, and affective displays are often themselves culturally coded. Practicing a few rounds of coding with members of your staff will allow you to refine the instrument and clarify discrepancies in application and potential frictions. You may also identify affective behaviors that don't seem readily categorizable with the instrument but seem important to the contingencies of that particular situation. I posit that the codes themselves are not as valuable as the conversations around display affect that they enable. The SPAFF as I've deployed it in this book went through three rounds of iterative coding before I applied it to the sessions in the next chapter. We found that the process of refinement offered as much for our staff as did the dedicated exercises themselves.

3. **SELECTION CRITERIA.** What is the most appropriate setting to consider this question? If it is a session, what criteria make it appropriate for study? If you're looking for more indicative examples of emotional labor, this may consist of how well the session was rated by the client. It may also be similar to Mankiewicz and Thomson's selection criteria wherein both tutor and student rate the session. Session length may

also be a consideration. For training exercises, for instance, drilling down on establishing rapport, agenda setting, or wrapping up a session may not require a full session's worth of data. Encouraging a tutor to consider their affective habits more broadly, however, may require several sessions from the same tutor. Other workplace environments may be of interest to you as well. Services encounters at the front desk or over the phone warrant their own forms of emotional labor, as do tutor-to-tutor interactions during staff meetings.

4. **SECURE PERMISSIONS.** Consult with your institution's IRB to determine how they interpret your project in terms of human research. Regardless of whether you need IRB permission, secure permission from the participants before recording. Inform them of what you're doing and why you're doing it.

5. **RECORD SESSION(S).** Although many, if not most, of the cues we identified tended to be verbal in nature, video recording is crucial for coding. In addition to the identifiable bits of facial gestures and body language, sometimes a visual "mood" alerted us to be more aware of what was transpiring in a session. Sometimes that mood provided the cues necessary to help us contextualize ambiguous behaviors (such as sarcasm, understatement, or other context-dependent information).

6. **TRANSCRIBE SESSION(S).** Once the session is recorded, it should be transcribed to enable participants to read along, code, and point to particular areas. For the sake of simplicity, we have favored simple turn-based transcriptions, though vertical transcription (Gilewicz and Thonus, 2003) could capture many of the conversational nuances and paralinguistic cues that often accompany affective exchanges (particularly around Validation cues such as backchanneling and sentence finishing).

7. **CODE ON TRANSCRIPTIONS.** Here it is important to watch along with transcriptions to observe nonverbal behavior such as what is described in Appendix A. I use the Comment feature in Microsoft Word to label instances of Affect. Sometimes this involves inserting a comment into a piece of dialogue where a participant makes a relevant face or gesture and describing it. This typically tends to involve backchanneling, an indicator of Validation.

8. **HAVE CONVERSATIONS.** For you and your staff, this may be a norming session for reliability. It may simply be, as it was for our center, an iterative process wherein we brought our initial codes and then discussed our differences and what we had missed, revising and adjusting as we went. Once this initial coding and conversation occurs, what conversations can you and your team have? What can you do with what you've learned?

Affection shows concern for others and facilitates rapport and bonding.

1. **CARING STATEMENTS.** "I want to make sure we're using your time well," "I hope your midterm goes well!"

2. **COMMON CAUSE STATEMENTS.** "For sure!" or "Oh, I know!" or "Same!"

3. **COMPLIMENTS.** "I really like your attention grabber!" or "This was really helpful."

4. **EMPATHY.** Examples may include things such as adapting the gestures or body language of the session partner or echoing the partner's verbiage.

Anger responds to perceived violations of the speaker's rights to autonomy and respect. It serves as a kind of "affective underlining" of displeasure and complaint, indicating that an interpersonal boundary has been transgressed.

1. **FRUSTRATION.**

2. **ANGRY "I-STATEMENTS."** "I am so angry!" or "I am so frustrated right now!"

3. **ANGRY QUESTIONS OR COMMANDS.** "Why?!" or "Why won't you edit this for me?!" "Stop!" or "I don't need help with that!"

Belligerence/Contempt either attempt to provoke Anger or emotionally harm, diminish, or humiliate others. While this could be directed at a tutor or writer, indicators can also be reserved for those outside the session: instructors, family, roommates, etc.

1. **TAUNTING QUESTIONS.** "Why?" (frequent and irritating).

2. **UNRECIPROCATED AND/OR HOSTILE HUMOR.**

3. **INTERPERSONAL TERRORISM.** "What would you do if I did?" or "What are you going to do about it?" "Don't interrupt me!" as a means of demonstrating power.

4. **CONTEMPTUOUS BEHAVIOR.** Sarcasm, mockery, insults, etc.

Criticism attacks someone's character (or writing) in a way that is not obviously insulting, as in Belligerence/Contempt.

1. **BLAMING.** "I received a D on that assignment because you didn't edit for me" or "You always add commas where you don't need them."

2. **CHARACTER ATTACKS.** "You guys never give me the feedback I really need."

3. **KITCHEN SINKING.** "Every time I come to the writing center, I don't get the help I want and no one listens to me. I failed my last paper."

4. **NEGATIVE MIND READING.** "You just think I'm stupid" or "You just don't get it because you're not in business."

Defensiveness functions to deflect responsibility or blame. It is often a face-saving mechanism.

1. **THE "YES, BUT."**

2. **CHANGING THE SUBJECT.**

3. **MINIMIZATION.** "Yes, the essay could be longer, but since it bleeds onto the third page, that technically makes it three pages, so it's fine" or "I don't care; I only need a C."

4. **EXCUSES.** "Well, the directions weren't clear, so there was nothing I could do."

5. **AGGRESSIVE DEFENSES.** "I did not!" This can often occur around assessments of potential plagiarism

Disgust is a relatively involuntary verbal or nonverbal reaction to a stimulus that is perceived to be noxious.

1. **INVOLUNTARY REVULSION.** This can sometimes be encountered in writing about medical conditions, lab reports, or other descriptive writing.

2. **MORAL OBJECTION.** Here the object of disgust is an action or idea that the speaker finds repulsive for moral or other symbolic reasons, as in responses to undesirable sexual practices or even political positions.

continued on next page

Domineering/Threats exert and demonstrate control over a partner or conversation.
1. **INVALIDATION.** "Oh, you are fine! Quit exaggerating" or "Your professor won't care about that."
2. **LECTURING AND PATRONIZING.** "Actually, your professor says . . ."
3. **LOW BALLING.** "You want me to get a good grade, don't you?" or "Do you want to pass the class?"
4. **INCESSANT SPEECH.** *It is a form of forcibly maintaining the conversational floor at all times.* Finger pointing, interrupting, negative sentence-finishing, etc.
5. **THREATS AND IF/THEN STATEMENTS.** "If I don't get a decent grade, I'm telling my professor you didn't help."
6. **GLOWERING.**

Enthusiasm expresses a passionate interest as well as a positive feeling or outlook associated with that interest.
1. **ANTICIPATION.** "Let's go!" "Let's get started!" or "I look forward to it!"
2. **INSPIRATION.** "I have a great idea now! Let me jot this down!" (with excitement).
3. **POSITIVE SURPRISE, EXCITEMENT, AND/OR JOY.**

Fear/Tension often involuntarily communicate fear, worry, anxiety, nervous anticipation, or dread. Often accompanies corrective feedback/critique.
1. **SPEECH DISTURBANCES.** Rapid uhs and ahs, possibly stuttering.
2. **VOCAL PITCH.**
3. **FIDGETING AND NERVOUS GESTURES.**
4. **NERVOUS LAUGHTER.**

Humor shares in mutual amusement and joy following a mutually recognized moment of absurdity or fun. It requires a moment of shared amusement.
1. **FUN, EXAGGERATION, WIT, SILLINESS.**
2. **GOOD-NATURED TEASING.** Self-deprecation is common here.
3. **SUDDEN GIGGLING.**

Interest communicates genuine interest in the session partner through active elaboration or clarification-seeking beyond mere information exchange.
1. **NONVERBAL ATTENTION WITH POSITIVE AFFECT.** Nonverbal behaviors leaning forward in their chairs, warm tone of voice, steady eye contact with *session partner or text*.
2. **ELABORATION AND CLARIFICATION-SEEKING.** Paraphrasing *questions* (Interest) are easy to confuse with paraphrasing *statements* that are coded as Validation (discussed later). "Was that frustrating for you?" "Am I understanding this correctly?"
3. **OPEN-ENDED QUESTIONS.**

Sadness refers to behaviors that communicate loss, resignation, helplessness, pessimism, hopelessness, or a plaintive or poignant quiescence.
1. **SIGHING.** Context can often determine whether to code sighing as Sadness or if it is simply neutral.
2. **POUTING/SULKING.** This can be expressed as a generalized reticence or annoyance. Pouting is often associated with thrust-out lips.
3. **RESIGNATION.**
4. **CRYING.**

continued on next page

TABLE 1.2.—*continued*

Stonewalling communicates an unwillingness to listen or respond to the receiver. 1. **ACTIVE AWAY BEHAVIOR.** Cleaning fingernails, looking at split ends or playing with common personal devices such as cell phones. 2. **NO BACKCHANNES.** (See Validation for backchannels.) 3. **MONITORING GAZE.** Stealing glances at their partners, as if to remind their partners to notice their lack of listening behavior.	**Validation** communicates sincere understanding and acceptance of one's partner or of one's partner's views and opinions. 1. **BACKCHANNELS.** Head nods and uh-huhs. Thumbs-ups can be common here. 2. **DIRECT EXPRESSIONS OF UNDERSTANDING.** "I agree" or "That's a very good point." 3. **PARAPHRASING.** "So if I understand correctly, you're saying . . ." 4. **APOLOGIES, GRATITUDE, AND THEIR ACCEPTANCE.** "I'm sorry" or "Thank you so much!" "It's okay" or "You're welcome." 5. **SENTENCE FINISHING, POSITIVE.**
Whining functions to make what might otherwise be an ordinary complaint into a plaintive or pleading form of emotional protest. 1. **VOCAL QUALITY.** High-pitched, nasal, sing-songy, or otherwise plaintive. For example, the question "why" might be expressed in a high-pitched voice and drawn out with an exaggerated "eeee" sound at the end, as in "whyyyyeeee?"	

In our initial round of coding and conversations, we hewed close to the language of the original SPAFF. That said, one of the earliest sticking points for us was that the original SPAFF divides affect into positive and negative cues. Like Morris and Concannon (2022), we immediately saw the importance in not "distinguishing between good and bad emotions and instead acknowledg[ing] the importance of how emotions are shaped, circulated, read, and interpreted" (xiii). Several of our tutors remarked that sometimes allowing for negative affect in sessions can be healthy: sometimes a writer is frustrated, and frustration often accompanies problem-solving when a student is truly challenged (D'Mello et al., 2010, p. 364). Sometimes a tutor is nervous about making a suggestion that may imply a great deal of work for the writer. Sometimes a writer may have experienced loss. In short, categorizing affect as positive or negative is only useful insofar as it helps us identify the particular affect. That said, some affects have no place in the writing center. Belligerence, contempt, and other bullying behaviors are destructive. Still, knowing what they are may help tutors identify them and respond meaningfully (as I will discuss in Chapter 4).

The codes make the behaviors observable and thus available for commentary. Staff training might emphasize roleplay scenarios in which tutors coach one another through how to encounter and navigate (and, if necessary, walk away from) these emotions as they arise in sessions.

Here I wish to emphasize that for training tutors, the abridged handout in Appendix B is likely sufficient as long as it is accompanied with meaningful training (more on this in Chapter 4). It is also crucial to understand that the indicators are not as important as identifying an instance as indicative of the affect itself. That is, rather than getting hung up on whether a particular display is a compliment or a caring statement, it should suffice to simply identify it as an instance of Affection. The SPAFF is based on a cultural informant approach, and thus it needs to be contextualized in the community of practice to which it is bound, alongside the various geographic and cultural inflections also acting upon it. What is "Midwestern nice," for instance, in one context may be perceived as passive aggressive in another. That isn't to say that the SPAFF is pointless and that observing affect is simply subjective. Rather, the SPAFF provides a framework for coders to proceed and evaluate emotional performance. It, like any other language, is a way to represent what we observe—a way to name what we feel.

Applying the SPAFF

In what follows, I apply our adapted SPAFF to a session to consider the role affect plays in a fairly typical writing center session. The findings of this section are not intended to be a prescriptive model of how consultants ought to comport their outward countenance during a session, nor are the results generalizable. As Lauer and Asher (1988) observed, "Qualitative descriptive research is often the first kind of empirical research done in fields that seek to identify the important aspects or variables of any phenomenon to be studied" (p. 23). As I have endeavored to explain in previous sections, writing center studies has long acknowledged that affect varies a lot in tutoring sessions. This case study thus attempts "to give a rich account of the complexity of writing behavior, a complexity that controlled experiments generally cannot capture" (Lauer & Asher, 1988, p. 45). This case thus represents a first effort at mapping some of the affective dimensions of the writing center session.

The session itself occurred at a Midwestern public university and was approved by the institution's IRB. The session was chosen among several recorded due to its typicality. Both participants felt the session was successful, and they were interviewed afterward and shown clips of the session to verify initial impressions. The SPAFF was applied after the iterative process described in the preceding sections.

CASE STUDY: KATE AND MARK'S SESSION

Synopsis of Tutoring Situation

Kate is a white female-identifying tutor in her third and final year at the writing center. Mark is a Black male-identifying student in his first year at the university. Mark had been to the writing center on other occasions but had not worked with Kate before. He is working on a first-year composition essay comparing his parents and their parenting styles, detailing his relationship with each. He has completed the essay, wanting feedback on clarity, concision, and correctness.

As Kate explained in the follow-up interview, they engaged in some small talk while the camera was being set up; consequently, the session begins with little of what we would normally consider rapport-building, but each conveys a warm affect: smiling and nodding as each asks questions and gathers information from the other. Kate asks Mark about the assignment and if he has a preference about who reads aloud. They decide to stop every paragraph or so to review. They then begin the general process of Mark reading aloud and Kate providing some feedback and asking questions, and then returning to the essay. Mostly Kate provides praise and then asks a follow-up question about Mark's choices in the paragraph. Based on his answer, she might provide some constructive criticism or advice. Mark is receptive to her feedback overall. They smile frequently in their interchanges between paragraphs, nodding and back-channeling each other to indicate they understand one another. The following is typical of the exchanges between the two.

> K: Okay . . . just a couple of things. I get how you have really, really good ideas and organization. Umm, the one [both laugh as they try to find what she's looking for] it's like in between the two pages. Umm . . . oh! You did hyphenate it. Okay, I missed that. Okay . . . why did you highlight this?
>
> M: Because I was wondering if I could leave this in there.
>
> K: Umm, I think it contributes to your voice quite honestly if I'm reading it.
>
> M: Okay.
>
> K: Umm, did your professor talk about, like, how academic, like, she wants, or she or he [both laugh]—I'm not sure—wants the voice?

M: Umm, no. I meet with her tomorrow at 2, so I can just ask her about it. Actually, I'll just highlight it, just . . . okay.

K: Okay . . . alright, umm . . . the other thing . . . umm the other page . . .

M: Oh! Sorry, oh yeah. Does this . . . this doesn't have to be copied, right?

K: No.

M: Okay.

They read through the brief essay during the session, and after Kate provides some organizational feedback encouraging Mark to reference the beginning of the piece to provide some form of closure, they review some of the formatting requirements of the assignment such as font and headers. Kate asks if Mark has any other questions as the session draws to a close, which he declines. They thank one another before Mark jokes, "Pray for me," as he packs up and departs. The session lasted roughly 40 minutes.

Applying the SPAFF to Kate and Mark's Session

Using our adaptation of the SPAFF, we can see the following overall count of affect instances during the course of the session.

Although Kate provides more instances of affect than Mark does, this is likely because Mark read from the essay and thus had fewer opportunities to emote. Overwhelmingly, Validation is the most demonstrated affect, and most of the indicators for it were in the form of backchannels: those head nods and uh-huhs people utter when someone else is speaking to demonstrate that they understand and accept what the speaker is saying. Mark demonstrated 37 instances of Validation, with 28 of those being backchannels. The remaining instances consisted of the following:

- paraphrasing Kate (1)
- directly stating that he understood her (1)
- apologizing (1)
- accepting a compliment (1)
- expressing gratitude (5)

Similarly, Kate demonstrated 42 instances of Validation, with 29 of those being backchannels. The remaining 13 instances of Validation consisted of the following:

- gratitude (1)
- accepting compliments or apologies (2)

TABLE 1.3. SPAFF Code Count of Kate and Mark's Session

Kate (Tutor) Affect Count	*Matt (Writer) Affect Count*
Affection: 14	Affection: 1
Enthusiasm: 1	Enthusiasm: 1
Fear/Tension: 2	Humor: 7
Humor: 4	Interest: 1
Interest: 7	Validation: 37 (28 backchannels)
Validation: 42 (29 backchannels)	

- finishing Mark's sentences (twice)
- direct statements of understanding (9)

For Mark, Humor was the second-most frequently appearing affect. I have coded Humor based on who initiates it. Per the SPAFF (and our adaptation), "Laughter or amusement that is not shared is never coded as humor" (Coan & Gottman, 2007, p. 277). Of these instances, most were typically self-deprecating or dry humor, though a few instances of exaggeration and playfulness appeared as well. Mark also showed Interest through elaboration and clarification-seeking, such as asking Kate, "How would I say 'most people'? I said 'the crowd' but does that make sense?" Finally, Mark showed an instance of Affection in the form of a compliment ("The last time I came here, I got a really good grade") and an instance of Enthusiasm (broadly smiling and saying "Okay! Yes!" after Kate affirmed that she understood some of his revision).

Kate demonstrates Interest six times throughout the session, primarily through questions and clarification-seeking. She often leans in as he reads, cocking her head to the side at parts as if trying to make sure she hears what he says correctly. She also demonstrates Humor four times through joking as well as wit and silliness. She demonstrates Enthusiasm once in the session at the beginning, exclaiming "Alright!" with a smile as they begin the session. Beyond Validation, Affection was the most common of Kate's affective displays. Compliments were by far the most common indicator, with one common cause statement ("Like, in my writing, I use the word *which* a lot" in response to Mark worrying he overuses certain phrases) and one Caring Statement ("Good luck on the last paper!") composing the others.

Finally, Kate displays two instances of Fear/Tension, each of which occur when she offers constructive criticism. For example, in response to Mark asking about using the word *crowd* to refer to most people, Kate bares her teeth a bit in a show of chagrin and inhales through them while she squints. Her pitch rises slightly as she rephrases his question and says, "Uh, it kind of makes sense. Like, I get what you're saying, but maybe something like 'makes her so popular' or something like that might be a better way to word that." In this exchange, her trepidation at negating his display of Interest is signaled by the facial expression and shift in vocal pitch, and it is quickly accompanied by a direct expression of understanding (i.e., "I get what you're saying") to minimize the potential negativity of saying "no" to his question. After he backchannels as she says this (signaling Validation), she follows up with a Validating statement of her own before offering a hedged restatement of her critique: "Your reader would definitely understand what you're saying, but I think there might be another way of saying that, maybe."

The second instance is similar and occurs after Mark reads his concluding paragraph. Kate offers a compliment (an indicator of Affection) before offering a critique on his writing: "Okay, good! I really like this part, and my only thing is are these last two sentences really addressing future parents since your audience is like . . . not addressing . . . it doesn't really address the audience. Is there a way that you could, like, think to change that?" During the critique portion, her pitch once again rises, and her face shows some hesitation. She also demonstrates what Coan and Gottman (2007) described as "speech disturbances" (p. 276), wherein she works through an incomplete few sentences trying to carefully phrase her feedback. It is perhaps also worthwhile to note that she seems to shift from saying "you're not addressing your audience" to "it doesn't really address the audience." The SPAFF code of Criticism is a complaint against someone's character. By shifting to "it" (the paper) rather than "you," Kate avoids seeming overly critical and demonstrates some nervousness as she navigates this rhetorical situation.

These displays mirror some of the negative politeness strategies Mackiewicz and Thompson (2013) identified in tutoring practices to minimize some of the potential face-threatening that can occur when tutors make suggestions or offer criticisms of the work. Kate's shift to "it" rather than "you," for instance, avoids "the pronoun *you* or impersonalize[s] the face-threat (e.g., a suggestion) by stating it in passive voice" (Mackiewicz & Thompson, 2013, p. 49). In fact, Mackiewicz and Thompson's (2013) five types of motivational scaffolding either overlap with or are facilitated by affective cues: praise, statements of encouragement or optimism, demonstrations of concern, expressions of sympathy and empathy, and reinforcement of students' feelings of ownership. Most of these constitute some form of Affection as defined by the SPAFF. And all are typically facilitated through the use of affective cues. In the previous examples,

Kate mitigates face-threatening acts through signaling her own discomfort. When Mark Validates her attempts, she Validates him in return.

As far as pacing, Validation was spaced fairly evenly throughout the session. The beginning of the session saw some Interest and Enthusiasm on the part of the tutor while they navigated the session agenda and the assignment. The end of the session featured a bit of Humor and Affection as well as Validation in the form of gratitude as they wrapped up and wished each other well. The bulk of the session's affective displays took place after Mark read a paragraph or so of his essay and invited Kate to respond. Returning to the earlier example of their exchanges with the SPAFF reveals some key features of their affective states throughout.

Kate opens with a compliment about Mark's organization and ideas (an indicator of Affection) and then jokes about her difficulty in finding a piece of the text she's looking for (an instance of Humor, which Mark shares by laughing). She asks why he highlighted a part (an indicator of Interest), and when he explains, she pays him another compliment about his voice. As she asks a closed-ended question about academic voice, she awkwardly stumbles in realizing she's assuming the gender of his instructor and laughs about it, which he reciprocates (Humor). He answers her question, and as he does so she nods and murmurs, "Mmm-hmm," backchanneling him (Validation). As she begins to consider the feedback she had about another item, he softly interrupts her with a closed-ended question, apologizing as he does so (Validation).

Although this session is not representative of every session, it is fairly typical. Validation—more than any other affect—seems to be the overwhelming mode of feeling in tutoring sessions. Validation is how participants communicate understanding and acceptance: about the writing at hand, the ideas being discussed, the revisions suggested, or the social niceties navigated whenever two people collaborate on a project. Backchanneling seems especially crucial in this session. Even when the other isn't looking—whether Mark is reading from his paper or Kate looks away while trying to explain a concept—each nods along to the other. For Hochschild (2012), exchanges such as these about paying respect and sincerely expressing gratitude—not only in our displays but in our feelings, "thus paying [our] debt in gold rather than in silver" (p. 77)—in actual feeling rather than the minimally expected gesture. Each session partner seems to actually feel like they are Validating their peer, whether or not that partner can perceive such Validation.

In fact, there are several points in the session when each person smiles or chuckles to themself, even when the other does not see it. While emotion can be performative, it is clear from Mark and Kate's exchanges that emotion is also *felt*. Micciche (2007) argued convincingly that "emotions are something we do rather than something we have," but these discrete instances of emotion—seemingly performed for no one—suggest that it is more than a Cartesian "I" (or we) "doing" emotion. Emotion is also experienced. Emotion may be performative, but as Giaimo (2024) has argued, it can also be reactive. Emotion, as Arrizabalaga et al. (2019) have argued, can "do" us. Tutors and writers are nodal points in the circulation of affect in writing center sessions, and the body is also a rhetor in these exchanges and can be attended to. Like teaching, tutoring is an embodied act. A close examination of affect and rhetoric in the session thus can reveal the complex interplay of subject and object, of the *who* "doing" rhetoric. Hochschild (2012) has explained emotion as "a sense that tells about the self-relevance of reality . . . Emotion is one way to discover a buried perspective on matters" (p. 85). Emotions speak to us. Tools like the SPAFF can help our tutors listen and make more informed choices in sessions based on that previously buried perspective.

Conclusion: Validation, Coin of the Affective Realm?

Fluency in affective cues can not only help us attend to what our bodies may be telling us, but we *can* use them to "do" emotion, to communicate how we wish to feel toward the other person: to help pay what we feel we owe, in Hochschild's (2012) terms. We can also be cognizant of a lack of cues. Abstaining from backchanneling, for example, may send a signal to the session partner that the listener doesn't accept or understand what is being talked about. This does not have to result from neglect, either. I am not prescribing that tutors should always backchannel writers; rather I think we need to begin understanding it as a feature of the peer tutoring genre. As Mannon (2021) has pointed out, conceiving emotion as labor rather than as simply a function of personality may enable tutors to make choices about whether or not to Validate their session partner's negative feelings (p. 163). Such a choice may help resist the traditional nurturing gender roles assigned to women tutors, enact minimalist tutoring strategies and thus protect the tutor's emotional reserves, and subtly indicate a refusal to cooperate with potential microaggressions.

In turn, tutors might note a lack of backchanneling in their session partner and use the opportunity to double-check that the listener understands or that they accept what is being discussed. They may also use it to become aware of their own failures to communicate or of microaggressions. This opens new opportunities for the session. Tutors may also use (or not use) backchanneling as a means to subtly signal to the writer that they are present and on board. In fact, among all of the cues, Validation seems to be the figurative coin of the realm in these exchanges: it signals whether one's rhetoric—on the page and in the conversation—is successful or not, a way to pay respect with "gold rather than silver." The SPAFF renders the minute and seemingly mundane exchanges in the tutoring session more visible and thus available for commentary. This case study demonstrates merely one way the SPAFF can be used to consider affect and emotion in the writing center session, highlighting especially the role Validation plays in "bowing from the heart" (Hochschild, 2012). This case study, however, also highlights several remaining questions and potential avenues for further research. For example, how are gender dynamics reflected in affective cues? How do hedging and humor function as affective strategies? How might the length of a session relate to the distribution of affect cues? These are just a few questions that can be taken up and developed in future research.

Finally, affect clearly plays a role in mediating several of the politeness strategies (both negative and positive) described by Mackiewicz and Thompson (2013) that in turn foster motivational scaffolding. As I work to demonstrate in the next chapter, this is not the only significant overlap between the codes of the SPAFF and instruments that have been developed to study the micro-level moves performed in writing center sessions. The SPAFF may help us understand the role affect plays in facilitating or frustrating these moves.

2

Affect, Collaboration, and Authority

In the prior chapter, I shared how my center adapted the SPAFF and applied the SPAFF on its own. In Chapter 4, I speak more directly to how I have used elements of it for the purposes of training. In this chapter, I look at a few writing center sessions using the SPAFF alongside codes developed in other studies to consider how the SPAFF may help us theorize the relationship between affect and other dimensions of tutoring writing. I focus especially on how affect may facilitate, anticipate, or result from common tutoring moves used in sessions as new tutors navigate collaboration and authority. Writing centers have long had an interest in exploring how tutors negotiate, exert, and/or mitigate authority in sessions (Carino, 2003; Corbett, 2011; Corbett, 2013; Hemmeter, 1994; Welch, 1995; Herman et al., 2020). As Corbett (2013), Carino (2003), Shamoon and Burns (1995), and others have found, tutors often struggle to navigate the directive/nondirective continuum. And though writing center orthodoxy has often needlessly vilified directive methods or conflated such methods with hierarchical thinking, one of the learning thresholds tutors must traverse is knowing how to navigate that continuum. New tutors, of course, often struggle to take on the persona of a qualified expert and assume that sort of authority. New tutors are thus an especially interesting case for emotional labor in that

https://doi.org/10.7330/9781646428649.c002

we can observe what these newcomers imagine the preferred affect display to be based on their training, their reading, and their assumptions.

As Mannon (2021) has observed, often

> our primary resources for training tutors have very little direct advice for performing this part of the job, perhaps because we perceive engaging writers' emotions to be an aspect of tutoring "that we can learn but that no one can simply teach us." (p. 165)

I am interested in how new tutors without direct training on affect use affect to navigate collaboration and authority in writing center sessions. What does the emotional labor of a new tutor trying to navigate collaboration and control look like?

Coding for Collaboration and Authority

To determine the sorts of collaborative moves made by new consultants, I draw primarily on Corbett's (2011) work in "Using Case-Study Multi-Methods to Investigate Close(r) Collaboration: Course-Based Tutoring and the Directive/Nondirective Instructional Continuum." Corbett's interest is in how course-based tutoring (CBT) participants negotiate instructional authority in the session, especially along directive/nondirective and control/flexibility continua. His framework synthesizes the work of Gilewicz and Thonus (2003), Black (1998), and Harris (1995) on rhetorical and conversational discourse analysis.

As Corbett (2011) explained, these sorts of analyses "offer broad rhetorical frameworks as well as ways to analyze linguistic features and cues from one-to-one tutorial transcripts" (p. 65). In particular, they offer ways to examine "macro-rhetorical issues to the micro-linguistic features and cues of one-to-one conferences" (Corbett, 2011, p. 66). As I will explain, these microlinguistic features include conversational moves like backchanneling, joint productions, interruptions, and more.

In short, these features provided the basis for codes to determine the relative degree of collaboration and directive/nondirective tutoring occurring in a given session. The appearance of these codes and their proximity to (or distance from) affective cues may help to theorize possible relationships between them. However, some of the collaborative codes overlap with the SPAFF codes. For example, collaborative codes such as backchanneling and sentence finishing (such as in Joint Productions) are indicators of Validation, and open-ended (as well as clarification-seeking) questions are indicators of Interest.

In the following case studies, I coded for the following, based on Corbett's (2011) codes:

- closed- and open-ended questions
- content-clarifying questions
- directive questions
- overlaps (interruptions, main channel overlaps, and joint productions)

Among the codes developed from Corbett's (2011) work, open-ended questions compose a broad category of question that requires more than a short or rote response (as opposed to closed-ended questions). As I will explain, however, I do not conflate open-ended questions with nondirective or superior tutoring practice. Indeed, closed-ended questions are often necessary for pumping and other forms of scaffolding (Mackiewicz & Thompson, 2013). I would argue, however, that their presence does provide some indication of new tutors' perceptions of preferred practices. Content-clarifying questions are those that ask the writer to clarify their topic or other content for the tutor; these, again, are privileged in writing center practice in that they assume a level of expertise in the writer that the tutor lacks, thus affirming some reciprocity and collaboration in the session. Directive Questions, on the other hand, serve a more directive and less collaborative function. For instance, "don't you think a comma belongs here?" is simply a way to phrase a command as a question.

Corbett (2011) drew on Gilewicz and Thonus's (2003) work to identify overlaps in conversation, which he defined as "any simultaneous speech in which a conversational participant takes the floor before the first speaker has relinquished it by what Jefferson calls 'completion intonation'" (p. 35). Gilewicz and Thonus (2003) enumerated three kinds of overlap. First, interruptions occur when a participant initiates a contribution to the conversation before the other participant has finished theirs. Second, main channel overlaps occur when "the person overlapping does not take or is not permitted to take the floor" (Gilewicz & Thonus, 2003, p. 36). In other words, whereas an interruption terminates the prior speaker's utterance, in a main channel overlap both participants continue to talk, neither ceding the floor. Third and finally, joint productions happen when participants finish each other's sentences: "Joint productions, more than interruptions or main channel overlaps, represent a movement toward greater solidarity and collaboration" (Gilewicz & Thonus, 2003, p. 63). Joint productions can often thus be an indicator of the sorts of collaboration tutors strive for in writing center sessions.

In addition to the codes derived from Corbett's (2011) study, as I analyzed the videos and transcripts, I also coded for other indicators of collaboration or authority that manifested in the sessions:

- unrelated questions
- imperative sentences
- qualifiers/hedging

For instance, I coded for questions unrelated to the writing as these often served a function in the rhetoric of the session, whether to reinforce rapport as participants talked about social events outside the center or as a way to redirect the session. I coded imperatives to see how often new tutors would simply tell writers what to do. I also counted the use of qualifiers as these emerged as a common tool among the novice consultants to engage in what they perceived to be nondirective tutoring. That is, they often used words or phrases that would soften criticisms or imperatives, such as "I might . . ." or "You probably want to. . . ." Finally, like Corbett (2011), I counted the number of words uttered by each participant, controlling for times when participants read aloud from the text. Then I determined the average number of words spoken per minute by each participant to ascertain who in the dyad was holding the conversational floor the most.

Once more, I am not claiming that these indicators are necessarily indicative of nondirective methods, nor do I claim that such methods are inherently superior to directive methods. That is, I do not claim that we should use this research to valorize the appearance of nondirective methods in a session. Instead, I am interested in attempting to map out how new tutors—who often struggle to navigate that very spectrum (Nicklay, 2012; North, 1994)—exchange affects with writers and navigate collaboration and authority. In short, I look at how these new tutors attempt to enact what *they* imagine the preferred affective display of the writing center to be, typically embodying a nondirective, collaborative ethos.

Finally, I do not assert that these codes transcend the contexts in which they are embedded, nor do I assert that the findings are generalizable. As with the SPAFF, however, counted instances allow for a more granular description than an otherwise more holistic observation might have. Further, the ability to count clusters of instances of affect and collaboration that might not otherwise have been perceived in temporal proximity has enabled me to consider potential relationships between the two. In short, examining the transcripts and recordings of the sessions with the SPAFF and collaborative codes have enabled me to consider how new consultants use affective display in order to produce Hochschild's (2012) "proper state of mind in others" (p. 7) for writing center work. That is, it has helped me to see what their emotional labor actually looks like.

In the analyses below, I capitalize observed affects (e.g., Validation) and italicize their indicators (e.g., *fidgeting*). Similarly, I capitalize observed collaboration codes (e.g., Open-Ended Question).

Two Case Studies

In this section, I look closely at two sessions from a small liberal arts institution in the Midwest to consider how two new tutors navigate emotional labor in their sessions. I chose these two sessions because they serve as a generative contrast in terms of how tutors emotionally labored in somewhat similar circumstances. As in the previous chapter's case study, each session was video recorded and transcribed before coding. After initial review, each session's participants were invited to participate in follow-up interviews. That institution's IRB approved the study. My hope is that the thick description of each session conveys its typicality. These are not peculiar writing center sessions but instead feature exchanges common to the genre.

Despite the differences in the sorts of affect and emotional labor in each, they shared several similarities with each other. First, the two sessions were roughly the same length, just under half an hour, and neither appointment was scheduled. Second, each of the student writers came to the center to address later-order concerns (LOCs). Third, each of the consultants was inexperienced and at the same level of training; that is, each was in his first semester in the role and in the midst of a one-credit writing center practicum course. Their primary text for the course was *The Bedford Guide for Writing Tutors*.

Despite these similarities, the two sessions provide a very productive contrast in how new consultants might manage affect and the negotiation of authority in the session. Observing the emotional labor of new tutors in particular can demonstrate how our disciplinary ethos is conveyed in the form of our training texts and embodied in our pedagogical practices. In other words, such a consideration shows how new tutors imagine what writing center emotional labor ought to look like as they learn the genre of peer tutoring.

I begin by sharing two brief narratives summarizing the sessions. I then revisit portions of the sessions with the codes to render a fuller description.

Based on these descriptions, I reflect on the relationship between collaboration and affect, noting that even in sessions that seem emotionally neutral, writing center practice is emotionally labor intensive. Finally, I assert that such labor recruits a fair amount of emotional intelligence. However, I caution that without some training in mindfulness and without rhetorical care, this emotional intelligence could be manipulative or cynical in its use. These strands will then be taken up more fully in the next chapter.

JAMES AND AMY'S SESSION: SYNOPSIS

James is a white male-identifying tutor in his third year at the college and in his first semester at the writing center. Amy is a white female-identifying student in her second year at the college. Amy came to the writing center looking for help with citations on a short extra-credit assignment about volcanoes for a geology class. She is primarily concerned with citing her online sources correctly. She also wants to make sure the paper reaches the bare minimum of the page-length requirement to get the extra credit. She and James were unacquainted prior to the session. After greeting each other and acknowledging the awkwardness of the camera and briefly laughing about it, they begin the session. Amy's laptop faces her, and she keeps a sheet of loose-leaf paper on hand to write notes. After a brief bit of small talk, James asks about what she cited and tries to get more information from her before reading out of the book and relaying the relevant citation information. She asks questions about how to identify the author and he answers. They proceed in this manner through the session by going through her citations one-by-one. After about 12 minutes, they arrive at the end of the citation list. James fills out one of the end-of-session forms while Amy reads one of her online sources, taking notes on the loose-leaf sheet of paper.

However, this is a false finish. At this point, James asks if she has any further questions, and Amy then asks about the order of the information in her citation. The session continues for another 12 minutes, and they settle into something of a pattern: she asks him a question about citation, and he answers. If his answer becomes too long, however, she interrupts and emphasizes the fact that her paper is for an extra credit assignment. This is especially the case when he offers suggestions for developing the paper a bit further. He then echoes her and finishes her sentences, and on one occasion he wrests the conversational floor from her. After a few exchanges like this, they finish the session at roughly 24 minutes in. After Amy jokes about only technically meeting the length requirement (a few lines on the fifth page), they say their goodbyes, ending the session. Amy rated the session highly in the post-session form, and on the surface it would appear to be fairly neutral in terms of emotional labor.

LAWRENCE AND KAYLEE'S SESSION: SYNOPSIS

Lawrence is a Black male-identifying tutor in his third year at the college and in his first semester at the writing center. Kaylee is a Black female-identifying student in her third year at the college. Unlike James and Amy, Kaylee and Lawrence were briefly acquainted prior to the session and have some friends in common. They also had one session prior to the one recorded. Accordingly, the level of rapport between them was quite evident at the beginning. Like Amy, Kaylee had come to the center for assistance with later-order concern (LOC) issues—primarily regarding citation—for an essay written for a class on Islam.

They begin by exchanging pleasantries, and much like James and Amy, they mug for the camera and joke over it. Lawrence begins setting the agenda for the session by asking Kaylee what her paper is about. She describes it and says she just needs to look over spelling and grammar, though Lawrence suggests that he wouldn't mind looking through the short paper quickly for other things. He asks about where in the writing process she is. They begin looking at citation and grammar issues in the essay. Repeatedly throughout the session, Lawrence's phone buzzes and they joke about it, given the presence of the camera. After each distraction, however, Lawrence refocuses the discussion, steering it with questions regarding higher-order concerns (HOCs) in the paper such as Kaylee's thesis or organization. After addressing those questions, the conversation returns to LOCs as well as shared anecdotes about writing in other classes and situations. At the conclusion of the session, they discuss weekend plans, and Kaylee catches an inconsistency in one of her citations. They quickly work through it, however, and wrap up the session. In follow-up interviews, both described the session as pleasant, and at a glance the session would appear to be friendly, warm, and engaged.

APPLYING THE CODES TO JAMES AND AMY'S SESSION

Revisiting James and Amy's session with the codes explained above reveals several patterns regarding affect and collaboration. In the beginning of the session, James and Amy exchange *common cause statement* indicators of Affection as well as *wit and silliness* indicators of Humor to address the initial awkwardness in the first minute of the session (particularly the presence of the camera). James begins asking *closed-ended questions* about the citations Amy provided.

James also offers Qualified suggestions that relied on the use of the second person in formulations such as "So what you probably want would be either the short word for a website or … I guess that's it" and "Yeah, so that's probably who you'd put for your last name for your in-text."

After the initial joking, Amy displays some physical cues associated with the affect Tension—such as *fidgeting* and widening her eyes while stretching her lips—when she assumes James isn't looking. At one point, she exclaims, "Alrighty, this one looks easier than the last!" while smiling and raising her eyebrows. Taken together, these indicate Enthusiasm (*anticipation* plus relevant physical cues). James, however, does not seem to notice her Enthusiasm and thus does not reciprocate, instead concentrating on the screen. Soon after, Amy settles into a pattern of asking short, *closed-ended questions* to which James offers short answers. James gives short advisory directives based on the handbook (which he retains control of throughout the session), which are often Qualified in language such as "If you want to, you can supply the URL at the bottom."

A typical exchange in the latter half of the session (after the false finish) involves Amy asking a Question (sometimes closed-ended, sometimes open-ended), James beginning to answer it, and Amy interrupting as he speaks. James would attempt to finish, leading to brief Main Channel Overlaps. During that overlap, Amy would attempt to explain her confusion or interject with another *question*. In one instance, James then commandeers the production with a long expository passage (an indicator of the affect Domineering) while Amy cedes the conversational floor, *backchanneling* James. In short, although there was not much overt tension in the session, they often subtly struggled for the conversational floor and authority in the session.

The following example is somewhat indicative of the latter portion of the session. The following transcription shows an instance where each works to control the conversation, followed by an explication of the affective cues contained therein.

15:18

J: You can't just have a huge run-on sentence [*widens eyes in exaggeration; gestures*]

A: [*laughs*] Yeah.

J: of information, you have to kind of split it up to signal

A: Yup.

J: you are

A: but if I find something in the text, but I already knew it like, just because I knew it, do I have to still cite it?

J: Uhm, usually what you want to do in the situation is if it's not common knowledge?

A: What if it's common science knowledge? [*nervous laughter*]

J: Um—well if it's common for your field then yeah, you don't need

A: Okay

J: to worry about it. But say if you're like if, you were writing a paper for like an Intersections class

A: And just like randomly knew

J: Yeah

A: something

J: Yeah, then you might have to

A: Well we've talked about it kind of in class, so I just kind of knew it so . . .

J: And like in those types of situations usually your professor, unless it's like a lot

A: Mmmhmm

J: of stuff like that, if it's just like one random thing, usually your professor will be like 'Oh I wonder if they got this from somewhere' and typically they will like write a note on your paper or ask you and if you explain it and they will understand.

A: Yeah, yeah . . . Yeah.

J: But situations like that, if it's something you already know beforehand, there's no sense in just like going to the internet being like okay I wonder if I could find

A: Mmhmm, okay

J: this online so I could just quote it.

Despite struggles for the conversational floor during the session, at the end of the session Amy and James share a brief affective exchange of Enthusiasm and Affection indicators such as *joy*, *empathy*, and *compliments*. These indicators are mirrored by James and Amy's shared smiles.

Still, at the end, James tries to offer some parting advice, but Amy negates it with a *minimizing statement* (an indicator of Defensiveness) followed by another question. James *compliments* her question (an indication of Affection) and answers it before they conclude.

Despite these subtle tensions, Amy rated the session quite highly in the satisfaction survey she took at the end of the session.

LAWRENCE AND KAYLEE'S SESSION

Similar to James and Amy's interactions at the beginning of the session, Lawrence and Kaylee's initial pleasantries are composed of several Humor and Affection indicators before Lawrence asks her what her paper is about and negotiates an agenda for the session. During the session itself, both consistently *backchannel* while the other speaks, an indication of Validation.

Whenever Lawrence's phone vibrates, they joke about it being caught on film, exchanging still more Humor and Affection indicators such as *good-natured teasing* as well as *wit and silliness*. Interestingly, after the first disruption, Lawrence seizes on the moment to redirect Kaylee from some of the LOCs they were discussing, pointing out where he is confused about the essay's content. She then explains her intentions while he Qualifies his confusion with an I-statement: "Oh I was just tryin' to . . . this stuff just confuses me."

She then invites his suggestions, and he *paraphrases* her as she talks through the issue, a Validation indicator. Their subsequent exchange demonstrates Lawrence's typical strategies for showing Validation:

> L: Okay. So what I think you're saying is that as, um, culture changes, so does marriage, right?
>
> K: Yup.
>
> L: Okay yeah. Umm . . . I would actually add that in there, as culture changes, so does marriage.
>
> K: Why can't I be this good of a writer sometimes. . . . As culture changes . . . maybe I make writing too hard.
>
> L: No! I actually enjoy reading your papers . . . I read three of them so far if I'm not mistaken.
>
> K: Yeah, you read that one, but—[*the phone buzzes again*]—he's gonna kill you. [*shared laughter*]

Here Kaylee *affirms* Lawrence's understanding (Validation: *direct expression of understanding*), and then Lawrence offers advice Qualified by an I-statement (as opposed to a more imperative mode such as "put that in there"). Kaylee in turn offers Lawrence a *compliment* (Affection) and makes a self-deprecating statement, which Lawrence then rebuts with a firm "no" before offering a *compliment* (Affection) of his own while bolstering his own ethos for that compliment ("I've read three of them so far"), a move that centers his own authority but in a way that Validates her work and ethos as a writer.

At that point, Lawrence's phone buzzes again and they exchange more Humor indicators about the misfortune of this session being recorded. Lawrence quietly jokes, "It doesn't help that I know you," eliciting more laughter from Kaylee. They refocus on the suggested edit, and as Kaylee writes the last notes on her paper, Lawrence cedes authority by offering a Qualifier, saying, "And then again, that's just a suggestion. You don't have to actually make the changes if you don't want to." Kaylee accepts the suggestion however, using the moment to talk about writing in her courses in general. She remarks about how the professor offered them resubmissions, so she might as well rewrite some of the essay (having already received a first draft grade). Lawrence picks up this conversational thread, leading them to a brief tangent about their experiences in writing intensive courses at the college. They talk about enjoying the opportunity to rewrite papers for those courses. At the end of that conversational thread, Kaylee *apologizes* for the tangent (an indicator of Validation), to which Lawrence responds, "No problem. It's a short paper, so we have all the time in the world," an *acceptance of an apology* indicator of Validation followed by a *caring statement* indicator of Affection.

After briefly refocusing on the paper, another tangent begins where they talk about concision and professors' preferences. Kaylee shares her observations, and Lawrence Validates them through *direct expressions of understanding, backchanneling,* and *paraphrasing.* His phone buzzes a few times more throughout the session, and they joke about it, exchanging still more Affection and Humor indicators. They vacillate between LOCs as well as clarity and organizational HOCs. Each displays Interest and Affection indicators at a steady rate throughout the session—especially *empathy mirroring* (Affection).

And though by and large the session demonstrates a great deal of positive affect and collaborative codes, Lawrence occasionally asserts authority subtly whenever Kaylee asks his opinion on something by saying things like "I have no problem with that," as though he were authorizing her decision or granting her permission. He uses this same verbiage when she asks about scheduling another session with him as well.

As they conclude the session, Lawrence asks her about her weekend and they joke about it, further reinforcing rapport through Enthusiasm, Humor, and Affection indicators. As they fill out some of the writing center forms, however, Kaylee notices an inconsistency in one of her citations. They work briefly together, sharing the handbook. She works through the problem while Lawrence limits his commentary to things he notices about the order of her entries and footnotes, and they arrived at a tentative solution (as he Validates her through *backchannels* and *direct expressions of understanding*). Kaylee wonders why CMS citation style works the way it does, and Lawrence again Validates her and offers Affection indicators like *common cause statements* and *compliments*. They conclude with yet another exchange of Humor and Affection indicators before she leaves.

COMPARISON: AFFECT CODES

In addition to the descriptions above, I have counted the codes for these case studies. Overall, the affect indicators in both sessions clustered at the beginning and end of the session as well as around pivotal moments when collaboration or authority were negotiated. However, the way each tutor navigated those pivotal moments were quite different.

Overall, despite the similarities in the length of the sessions, there were far more instances of affect in Lawrence and Kaylee's session than in James and Amy's. To account for the small difference in time—Lawrence's session was roughly 3 minutes longer than James's—I have averaged the number of instances by the minute. Lawrence and Kaylee averaged significantly more demonstrations of affect than did the other dyad—both overall as well as averaged for minutes. Lawrence and Kaylee also did not demonstrate any negative affect. James, on the other hand, displayed one instance of Domineering (by way of the indicator *incessant speech*) to commandeer the conversational floor as demonstrated in the earlier example. Amy demonstrated two instances of Tension (through physical indicators such as biting her lip and/or the insides of her cheeks, a few instances of Defensiveness through *minimizing statements*, and nine instances of Domineering through *interruptions*).

Regarding positive affects, James demonstrated 3 instances of Humor, 8 instances of Affection, 17 of Validation (5 of which were *backchannels*), 1 instance of Interest, and 1 of Enthusiasm. Amy displayed 3 instances of Humor, 3 of Affection, 34 instances of Validation (26 of which were *backchannels*), 1 instance of Interest, and 3 of Enthusiasm. As seen in the examples above, most of the positive affects were exchanged at the beginning and end of the session, whereas the Domineering affect (as well as most of the *backchannels*) occurred

TABLE 2.1. Comparative SPAFF Code Count Between Two Sessions

Comparative affect	James/Amy	Lawrence/Kaylee
# of positive affect indicators	30/44	69/62
Avg. # of positive affect indicators/minute	1.24/1.82	2.5/2.25
# of negative affect indicators	1/13	0/0

TABLE 2.2. SPAFF Code Count, James and Amy's Session

James affect count	Amy affect count
Affection: 8	Affection: 3
Enthusiasm: 1	Enthusiasm: 3
Humor: 3	Humor: 3
Interest: 1	Interest: 1
Validation: 17 (5 backchannels)	Validation: 34 (26 backchannels)
Domineering: 1	Tension: 2
	Domineering: 9
	Defensiveness: 2

TABLE 2.3. SPAFF Code Count, Lawrence and Kaylee's Session

Lawrence affect count	Kaylee affect count
Affection: 9	Affection 8
Enthusiasm: 4	Enthusiasm: 1
Humor: 7	Humor: 10
Interest: 8	Interest: 15
Validation: 42 (22 backchannels)	Validation: 28 (16 backchannels)

at points where the conversational floor was being contested or when Amy resisted one of James's suggestions.

During his session, Lawrence displayed 7 instances of Humor, 9 of Affection, 42 instances of Validation (22 of which were *backchannels*), 4 instances of Enthusiasm, and 8 of Interest. Kaylee demonstrated 10 instances of Humor, 8 of Affection, 28 instances of Validation (16 of which were *backchannels*), 1 instance of Enthusiasm, and 15 of Interest. Similar to James and Amy's session, there were clusters of positive affect displayed at the opening and closing of the session. In Lawrence and Kaylee's session, however, affect was more evenly distributed throughout. At various points in the session where collaboration was negotiated, both Lawrence and Kaylee demonstrated several affect cues to soften suggestions through Validation and Affection.

TABLE 2.4. Comparative Collaborative Codes

Features and cues	James/Amy	Lawrence/Kaylee
Session length	24:14	27:35
Total words spoken	1879/887	1227/2490
Avg. # of words/minute	77/36	44/90
Backchannels	5/26	22/16
Closed-ended questions	12/20	6/18
Open-ended questions	3/3	4/5
Directive questions	1/0	2/1
Unrelated questions	0/0	1/9
Imperatives	2/0	1/0
Qualifiers	12/0	3/0

COMPARISON: COLLABORATION AND AUTHORITY CODES

Regarding the collaborative codes that emerged, as was likely obvious from the descriptions, Lawrence and Kaylee's session demonstrated far more indicators of what practitioners might consider a more collaborative session. That said, collaboration manifested in both sessions in different ways.

Following Corbett's (2011) method, I counted and averaged the number of words spoken by each participant (removing words read aloud from the student's text) to get a sense of who tended to control the conversational floor. Overall, the examination reveals two different approaches to navigating collaboration and authority by new tutors: James's approach was marked by qualifying and hedging in an attempt to mitigate authority while asserting it through speaking more and controlling the material resources at hand; Lawrence's approach was marked by mitigating authority through affective cues while asserting it through subtly steering the collaboration toward the tutor's areas of concern and how praise is phrased.

As the above table demonstrates, James spoke more than twice the number of words that Amy did during their session, whereas during the other session, Kaylee spoke twice as much as Lawrence. It seems that whichever dyad member spoke less in the session had more opportunities to *backchannel*, nodding or uttering affirmatives ("uh huh," "okay") while the other held the conversational floor. In both sessions, the student asked more Closed-Ended Questions than the tutors, typically to ensure clarity: "Does that make sense?" or "Is that confusing?" Lawrence's Directive Questions in the sessions were stated in such a way as to, as Corbett describes, "lead tutors . . . to their appropriation of one-to-one tutorials" (65). For example, while negotiating the agenda for the session, Kaylee asserted that she "just want[ed] to go over it for errors, like spelling," Lawrence asked, "You sure? We can look at it if you want." Kaylee then responded, "It's up to you," thus ceding some of the authority to Lawrence in response to the question.

Similarly, James used a Directive Question to steer the direction of the session, asking Amy if she could open up a web page in a new tab so they could look at the site she was citing. He then followed the question up with an Imperative sentence marked by a Qualifier (which is often an attempt to soften the tutor's authority): "Try references, maybe . . ." to steer Amy toward a different page on the website. Similarly, at one point in his session, Lawrence said to Kaylee, "Don't forget your [garbled word, likely *pencil*], too, that way if you see something you would like to mark up. . . ." Both instances indicate how Imperatives were used more to direct the agenda and modalities of the session (pencil, website) rather than the actual writing in the sessions. Each mitigated their Imperative sentences with words or phrases like *maybe* or explanations like "that way . . ."

James used far more Qualifiers and hedges in his talk compared to Lawrence. Like in the instance above, James not only used Qualifiers more frequently but in such a way that was sometimes at odds with the feedback offered. For example, at one point while prompting the student to properly cite a website, he said, "So what you probably want would be either the short word for a website or . . . I guess that's it." Similarly, he told her, "So after the article you would put, probably, just 'geology.com.'" On the one hand, these could be seen as uncertainty on his part—being unsure about how to properly format the citation. On the other hand, as he explained these items, he pointed to places in the handbook they're using to demonstrate his evidence. Instead, it seems that there was no linguistic or semantic need for the "probably" Qualifier in these instances. Rather, he seemed to use the Qualifier as a means of softening the authority he assumes in making these recommendations. Similarly, he sometimes softened a request with a Qualifier, such as when he said, "And if you don't mind, I'll just double-check over this." In the absence of many overt instances of positive affect or collaborative cues, James thus seemed to rely on qualifiers as a means of enacting what he perceived to be the nondirective "preferred countenance" of a writing center tutor.

Of course, peer tutoring is a material and embodied genre, so the environment and its effects also facilitated collaboration in other ways. For instance, James kept hold of the APA handbook they were using while Amy had her paper and laptop in front of her. Consequently, he tended to act as a gatekeeper (intentionally or not) for answers needed from that resource. Conversely, he would either ask Directive Questions or make an Imperative to elicit cooperation from Amy whenever her laptop was required to look at her online sources. For instance, at one point, when the sun began glaring on her screen, he asked, "Sorry, do you think we could move your laptop?"

Interestingly, material disruptions to the work of the session affected both the collaborative and the affective tones of both sessions. In James's session, sunlight coming through the large windows created glare on Amy's screen, leading James to apologize in a request to move, which led to her validating his perceptions about the glare through direct *expressions of understanding* and still more *backchannels*. In short, the disruption led to mutual Validation in the midst of what was otherwise an affectively neutral spell in the session.

In Lawrence's session, the phone served as a distraction that was in many ways productive: the exchange of Humor and Affection indicators that followed each clearly demonstrated a strong rapport between the tutor and writer. What's more, in a kairotic display of emotional intelligence, Lawrence seized on the distraction and subsequent rapport to shift the focus of the session from the LOCs in citation that Kaylee was interested in to the HOCs he perceived in Kaylee's organization and clarity. In short, he used the disruptions to steer the collaboration toward what he felt were more pressing issues, mediating that direction through affective cues such as Humor, Validation, and Affection.

Affective Approaches to Collaboration and Authority

It is impossible to generalize two case studies, yet these sessions demonstrate how vital affect and conveying the "preferred countenance" are in facilitating collaboration in the writing center session. Similarly, it may be too reductive to assume causation—or even correlation—about whether the positive affect indicators prompted the collaborative cues or if successfully fostering collaboration allowed for more positive affect. There are, however, several similarities across both sessions that can contribute to theory-building.

The sessions show that even relatively new consultants perceived a preferred display affect—an "outward countenance"—for the writing center and worked to embody and enact that countenance. The abundance of positive affects at the beginning and end of both sessions demonstrates the importance of rapport in writing center sessions, and how tutors and writers work to achieve it through verbal and embodied emotional labor. Both sessions featured a great deal of Humor, Affection, and Interest cues at those vital points. Both sessions also demonstrate the emotional and felt tensions inherent in writing center work: between the expertise of a tutor and the nondirective ethos specific to the center.

For instance, James did not Validate Amy during the session as much as Lawrence Validated Kaylee. In lieu of that, James often softened his feedback and instruction with Qualifiers, but he still maintained control of the citation style handbook. Similarly, Lawrence's use of affect to smooth over direct assertions as well as cessions of authority convey the same. Though both sessions show striking differences in the use of affect and authority, both sessions demonstrate how collaboration and authority in the sessions were mediated through affect indicators: Validation, Humor, Affection, Interest, and others.

Rather than asserting that one session or approach is better than the other, I want to consider how each tutor responded to the particulars of his rhetorical situation and navigated collaboration and authority through his emotional labor. James did not know Amy prior to her session with him, and as the session proceeded, it became clearer that she had fairly firm boundaries around what sorts of feedback she would accept. Rather than deeming their session less collaborative, I would say that James responded to the situation with the tutoring and affective "moves" he had at hand. In the practicum, he was taught the importance of the writer's ownership of the text and ideas. When he faced resistance, he relied on direct explanation more than affect. His withdrawal may be itself a form of emotional labor. As Mannon (2021) has suggested, "regarding affective engagement as labor rather than as a function of personality means that tutors can deploy it purposefully—or choose not to" (p. 163). James identified early in the session that Amy's extra credit was riding on a technicality. That is, as Amy joked, "I mean I could ask, like, more questions on how to make it longer, but I don't really care. It's all on the fifth page and he said it had to be five pages, so you know I figured if it was touching the fifth page, it was good." Immediately, then, James's and Amy's goals for the session were different based on their positioning in the session and within the university. Amy's goal was not to improve her writing but rather to do the minimum necessary to get her extra credit. For her, this was bound up in making sure the explicit criteria for the credit were met: correct formatting and meeting the minimum page requirement (on a technicality).

James's purposes were somewhat at odds with Amy's. If her paper wasn't accepted because it hadn't actually met the intended page length, he may have worried about feeling responsible. He had also been taught to privilege higher order concerns through the writing center practicum texts such as *The Bedford Guide for Writing Tutors* and in his practicum meetings. As his director, I had worked to help him and his classmates understand that work on LOCs was also important, but the sheer amount of material in the course teaching him how to focus on HOCs had clearly prevailed in this particular instance. What's more, given the circumstances of this particular session—he was being observed by his supervisor—he had the added pressure of performing what he believed to be the preferred outward display despite the occasional resistance of his session partner. He attempted to soften and qualify some of his advice and authority at times despite the awkward nature of that mediation. Had he not been observed, he may have felt less pressure to enact what he perceived to be a nondirective session, but that presence nonetheless affected the session. In brief, the expectations of the instructor and the writing center director indelibly shaped the ways each participant was able to affectively be in the session and thus the nature of their emotional labor as well. He had to balance conflicting impulses while at the same time guarding his own emotional reserves (this phenomenon will be discussed more in the next chapter).

By contrast, Lawrence's acquaintance with Kaylee outside of the writing center had enabled him to privilege a different approach to collaboration and authority. While the codes demonstrate that both he and Kaylee were more affectively present in the session, and while they would indicate a far more collaborative session, Lawrence demonstrated a certain savvy about directing the session. His acquaintance with Kaylee outside of the session clearly influenced his affective performance in the session, allowing him to enact many of the tutoring moves associated with collaboration and reinforcing rapport through collaborative cues. Still, Lawrence demonstrated remarkable emotional intelligence in steering the collaboration. His verbal assertions of authority were subtle ("I have no problem with that") and often couched with positive affective, such as smiling warmly while saying he'd read many of her papers, or through *common cause statements* about the value of revising papers in other courses.

That the affective performances of the new tutors in the case studies I've shared above vary so widely affirms some of Mannon's (2021) claims about the assumed emotional intelligence of new tutors. I can't help but wonder how James's experience as a tutor in that situation might have been different had he developed some fluency in Validation cues and/or in reading some of the cues Amy displayed—even if only to be more present in making decisions about withholding those cues. Mannon (2021) has asserted that "direct and routine discussions of emotional labor provide vocabulary for more specific conversations with writers and tutors and a reassessment of the emotion work built into assumptions about the writing center" (p. 162). I believe the case studies I've shared in this chapter demonstrate that emotion work pervades even the most seemingly neutral sessions. Accordingly, a much more robust vocabulary can help us better identify that work.

3

Burnout, Guilt, and Cynicism in the Writing Center

If the previous chapters examined surface-acting behaviors and their relationship to collaboration in writing center sessions, this chapter considers the toll of that emotional labor. This is especially crucial because workers who tend to fake or suppress their emotions to follow feeling rules can experience further stress and burnout as a result (Grandey, 2000; Zapf, 2002). As Maslach and Leiter (2016) explained, burnout can encompass three dimensions: "overwhelming exhaustion, feelings of cynicism and detachment from the job, and a sense of ineffectiveness and lack of accomplishment" (p. 103). Based on the responses, while I examine all three dimensions, I focus most especially on cynicism. Although Maslach et al. (2001) and other researchers basing their examinations on Maslach's constructs have defined cynicism as "a negative, callous, or excessively detached response to various aspects of the job," (p. 399) I conceive it differently in this chapter, locating it alongside guilt as a necessary byproduct of the affective exchanges that occur in and intersect upon the writing center session.

The exigence for this chapter emerged from trying to understand my own staff's struggles with guilt. Of all the negative feelings associated with burnout, guilt is the one emotion that I have seen most frequently. That is, my tutors often reference feeling guilty when a session doesn't quite go the way they

https://doi.org/10.7330/9781646428649.c003

wished it had—perhaps they had difficulty prompting a writer to share more about their choices or perhaps they felt overly directive in a session. Sometimes that guilt manifests as imposter syndrome—thinking they are unequipped to meet the expectations of their role. These descriptions echo Hochschild's (2012) descriptions of guilt: "Guilt or worry may function as a promissory note. Guilt upholds feeling rules from the inside: it is an internal acknowledgment of an unpaid psychological debt" (p. 82). Guilt, then, comes from a misalignment between feeling, performance, and the expectations of the performance. Guilt's relationship to burnout has been discussed in a number of studies in management (Chu et al., 2012; Spencer & Rupp, 2009) and teaching (Chang, 2009; Hargreaves & Tucker, 1991; Prawat et al., 1983). Beyond a few recent articles, however, guilt seems somewhat absent in writing center literature.

For example, in "Got Guilt? Consultant Guilt in the Writing Center Community," Nicklay (2012) explored the concept of tutor guilt through interviews and close reading of some foundational writing center texts. Nicklay (2012) explained that her examination "revealed that guilt originates in how the writing center community is situated within the larger university and how an individual writing center community is structured" (p. 15). In particular, she found that her respondents

> indicated that they most often felt guilt for being directive in sessions focused upon lower order concerns, but all also indicated . . . that directivity was an appropriate method to use in those very same sessions. In other words, tutors felt guilt for using a method they realized was appropriate. (Nicklay, 2012, p. 22)

Those tutors perceived an implicit set of rules emphasizing nondirectivity that placed them at odds with the perceived needs of a given session.

Dixon (2017) modeled her research on Nicklay's (2012), also finding tutor guilt to be the result of confusion around their practice, believing "that these anxieties remain, not because of a lack of clear training or scholarship on the topic, but because tutors (and perhaps their directors) are conflating the concept of student-centeredness with the concept of non-directivity" (Dixon 2017, p. 7). Although directive tutoring methods have been destigmatized in recent years, the student-centered approach philosophically valued by writing centers is often mistakenly conflated with nondirectivity. Dixon's and Nicklay's studies have thus found that perceived pressures from outside the session—such as the (real or imagined) expectations of their directors or of faculty members, or navigating their own assessment of writer needs versus the perceived rules of the peer tutoring session—can pull tutors in seemingly different directions, resulting in guilt over being too directive or not helping the student enough.

Nicklay's (2012) and Dixon's (2017) work is especially valuable for demonstrating the disconnect between tutor and director perceptions of valued writing center practices. Whereas directors may work to establish that more directive methods in sessions are often effective and pedagogically sound, tutors may not share the same perception. However, I wonder if in limiting our discussion of guilt to institutional or strictly pedagogical contexts, we miss out on other factors that contribute to—or are caused by—tutor guilt. When we assume that tutors feel guilty due to a failure to align their practice with their perception of the center's mission, we may oversimplify the issue somewhat.

The questions, for example, that structure the interviews in Nicklay's (2012) study were limited to comparisons between principles and theories and the directive and nondirective binary. More crucial, however, is that Nicklay's and Dixon's examinations at base assumed an always already service-oriented tutor whose guilt is bound up in failing to achieve the organization's goals and values rather than their own. In this paradigm, the tutor's individual goals are assumed to be in complete alignment with the prosocial goals of the writing center: that is what the instrument of the study was measuring. This, in turn, is problematic because as Harris and Ogbonna (2002) explained, "although innumerable texts prescribe successful management approaches to improving service encounters, such research is largely premised on the assumption of a complaint, malleable, and submissive workforce" (p. 163). Although most writing center practitioners would likely not characterize a writing center session as a service encounter, the core assertion still holds true: writing center researchers cannot assume a tutoring staff whose interests and objectives are the same as the center's. Indeed, if researchers and directors understand the value of underlife and of the diversity of emotional subjectivities in the writing center, I would argue that we should actively resist such an assumption. In short, though I agree with Nicklay's (2012) and Dixon's (2017) findings—particularly those that acknowledge the role of the institution in fomenting tutor guilt—I want to broaden their consideration.

Although the disconnect between employee practices and an organization's principles can illustrate some aspects of emotional labor in sessions, there is much more to emotional labor than guilt in how it is situated in and inflects writing center practice. In short, a broader approach to the examination assumes that emotional labor in the writing center comes from managing incongruence. In writing center practice, there are myriad incongruences:

between tutors' goals and needs and their perceptions of the goals and needs of their writing center; between tutors' goals and needs and their perceptions of the goals and needs of writers; between writers' goals and needs and their perceptions of their rhetorical situation; between writers' goals and needs and writing center pedagogy; and still more. I find two incongruences to be especially pertinent in the focus group interviews. First, tutors often feel they don't have enough emotional resources to be as present in some sessions as they feel they ought to (especially during busier times in the semester). Second, tutors often feel that the social justice orientation of writing center pedagogy can place them at odds with the situations they find themselves in during their sessions.

Interestingly, guilt does not appear in the SPAFF, though it may be associated with the functions of some of the codes. For instance, Fear and Tension cover worry, and Sadness covers loss. Accordingly, rather than observing it in sessions, other methods may be more appropriate to understand the feeling and its relation to "feeling rules from the inside." I thus use the focus group interview testimonies to understand how this incongruence can lead not only to guilt but to a form of cynicism as well.

Focus Group Testimonies

There is a wealth of empirical research in other fields on emotional labor and its relationship to a myriad of related constructs such as emotional intelligence, surface and deep acting, emotional exhaustion, depersonalization, as well as personal accomplishment and satisfaction. In addition to these constructs, I was also interested in guilt, which Chang (2009) linked to burnout as well. I arranged for several focus group interviews to better understand tutors' articulated experiences in regard to these phenomena. As Smithson (2008) observed,

> Focus groups are not simply a means of eliciting knowledge from participants, but are often reported to be quite creative experiences for the participants themselves. . . . Groups can become a space for participants to discover new things about their condition or organisation, or to make contact with other people with similar experiences. (p. 361)

I felt this was a particularly important methodological approach given the topic. My hope was that in constructing narratives about their working lives, my tutors would also create means of addressing those narratives and advocating for themselves.

This research took place at a large Midwestern state university's writing center with the approval of that institution's IRB. To ensure honest answers from writing center employees who may have been intimidated to reply to some of the questions in my presence as the director, instead, a research assistant recruited subjects, facilitated and recorded the interviews, and transcribed the interviews. To ensure that the subjects remain anonymous to me as their director, the assistant collected consent forms and placed them in a sealed envelope kept for IRB review. Identifying information in the transcripts was de-identified and/or removed, and the audio recordings were destroyed. The only identifying information in the transcripts indicates the subjects' level of experience at the center (e.g., in-training, second year, third year, etc.).

The first focus group consisted of three members, the second consisted of four members, and the third consisted of five members. In part, the composition of these focus groups was a result of availability and scheduling. As Ritchie et al. (2003) observed, groups smaller than four can lose some of the qualities associated with being a group; however, they also acknowledge that groups of two and three can serve as a hybrid of focus group and in-depth interviews. That said, we hoped that scheduling a number of these interviews would not only expand our overall sample size but also give us several group dynamics to consider, with other group narratives emerging in the data. I also wish to acknowledge Smithson's (2008) observation that "sample populations in the focus groups are small and non-representative. Topics are not all discussed in equal depth in all groups" (p. 362). Accordingly, I treat these groups as "collective testimonies" (Madriz, 2000), contextualizing and situating larger workplace constructs of emotional labor in the stories told by tutors themselves.

I divided the focus group interview script into areas based on the constructs developed by Lee and Ok (2012) in their study on the relationship between emotional intelligence, emotional labor, and burnout in the hospitality industry. This study examined how emotional intelligence correlates with emotional labor behaviors and with dimensions of burnout. Lee and Ok (2012) found that emotional intelligence tended to correlate with emotional effort—or deep acting—and accordingly with high levels of personal accomplishment and job satisfaction. Conversely, they found that emotional dissonance—often synonymous with surface acting—tended to correlate with depersonalization and emotional exhaustion.

I thus used this study's constructs to structure the focus group interviews because I felt they would help me to understand guilt and/or related feelings of burnout among tutors and to theorize the relationships between these constructs in writing center work. Regarding emotional intelligence, I wanted to see how tutors described monitoring and regulating their emotional states and the emotional states of others. I felt that patterns emerging in the data in this area might help make some sense of patterns that emerged in the questions regarding surface and deep acting. I wanted to see if the answers given regarding surface acting were linked at all to exhaustion and depersonalization or, conversely, if deep acting contributed to a sense of accomplishment or job satisfaction. Finally, I wanted a sense of how guilt may or may not be bound up in these larger questions and so that received its own section of question. Although I provided the research assistant with sample questions under each area, I instructed him to let the conversation play out organically and use the questions to facilitate conversation rather than presume a need for highly structured questions and answers. A sample interview script can be found in Appendix C.

Perhaps the biggest weakness of the study is ironically due in part to the anonymity of its participants. That is, given the subjects' anonymity, I have no way of knowing if a given speaker in an interview identified as non-majority, whether in terms of race, sexuality, or another category of intersectionality. I worry that this might not only whitewash the data but also fail to consider how women and people of color pay what is sometimes referred to as an "emotional tax" in the workplace. According to a report assembled for the nonprofit organization Catalyst, people of color report paying an emotional tax by being on guard against the race bias or gender bias they encounter in the workplace. As researchers Travis and Thorpe-Moscon (2018) defined it,

> Emotional Tax is the combination of feeling different from peers at work because of gender, race, and/or ethnicity and the associated effects on health, well-being, and ability to thrive at work. These experiences can be particularly acute for people of color who fear being stereotyped, receiving unfair treatment, or feeling like the "other" (i.e., set apart from colleagues because of some aspect of their identity such as gender, race, or ethnicity). While most experiences of otherness are detrimental, a lifetime of being marginalized can have uniquely potent effects, including on health and well-being.

Obviously, then, the emotional tax paid by women and people of color would play a significant role in emotional labor and burnout among tutors. Accordingly, it is difficult to assess the crucial role identity and intersectionality play in the testimonies offered by research participants in this study. Given my findings on guilt and cynicism among what are presumably majority tutors, I can only assume that this experience is thus heightened among women, people of color, and LGBTQ+ people in the center.

Finally, because I am not studying the linguistic features of the subjects' utterances, I did not transcribe the interviews vertically and they are instead straightforward renderings to capture intelligibility rather than accuracy. There are, for example, no instances of stammering, stuttering, or similar linguistic features. However, I have chosen to keep the backchanneling and other forms of affirmation present in the transcriptions, and these will occasionally be represented in the excerpts that follow. I have done so because of how this behavior indicates that one subject's sentiment is shared by those others in the group, that their words are indeed indicative of a collective testimony.

Surface Acting, Deep Acting, and Level of Experience

As I explained in the introduction of this book, surface- and deep-acting behaviors are how emotional labor is embodied and enacted. Surface acting denotes behaviors at odds with one's feelings to enact the perceived proper display for a given situation. In contrast, deep acting refers to when one works to change one's feelings to match the expectations of the situation, whether policies, relationship expectations, organizational goals, and so on.

SURFACE-ACTING BEHAVIORS

Several themes and commonalities emerged across focus groups regarding surface-acting behaviors and the situations that occasion them. Some tutors reported surface acting to mimic empathic behaviors with writers who came in for help on a paper "at the last minute" or with writers whom they happened to dislike or who were rude due to not receiving the sort of help they desired. Most described surface acting in showing excitement or eagerness in sessions when the writer appeared uninterested or unengaged. For instance, one tutor described a weekly appointment with such a writer:

> I worked with a writer last semester who wasn't very focused on their writing, uh, expressed not wanting to really be at the appointments all the time, and—I . . . kind of had to do a lot of cajoling of, like, c'mon, you know, we just got to get through this, like, your paper will improve because of this, like, I know you want to be a stronger writer. And, doing a lot more of that . . . um . . . kind of like, c'mon, you know, just play the game, play along. Like, you know, I can't really force you to be here, but I don't want to see you fail.

In this response, the tutor demonstrates their emotional labor in enacting Thompson and Mackwiez's (2014) motivational scaffolding strategies such as using the inclusive "we" form and giving reasons to "explain the payoff" (p. 51). But perhaps more interestingly, this approach—emphasizing "playing the game"—indicates that the tutor acknowledges the preferred behaviors typically associated with the session to the writer as well. Returning for a moment to the notion of cynicism, the tutor recognizes that each has a role to play in this affective exchange; it is a "game" wherein the participants play the parts in exchange for the outcomes: grades for the student ("I don't want to see you fail") and a conservation of emotional reserves for the tutor.

Scaffolding strategies also appeared more broadly in the subjects' responses to questions about surface-acting behaviors. Tutors were savvy about the need at times to affect a certain disposition or stance to facilitate scaffolding. For instance, several remarked on adopting a certain level of naïvety or ignorance about a subject (like citation styles, word processing software, etc.) to encourage the writer's self-efficacy and reinforce the writer's ownership of the text. Others reported relying heavily on praise, encouragement, and similar motivational scaffolding strategies, regardless of whether they felt the writing (or writer) warranted those behaviors or if those moves felt genuine to them.

Similarly, tutors reported surface acting in response to writers negatively commenting on their professors, their classes, or their own writing. One tutor explains,

> I think, like, specifically in sessions—in sessions where the writer keeps ragging on themselves, like, ah, I'm such a bad writer, I'm just so terrible at this. It's like, I feel like—usually I don't feel like I have to put on a mask, but, like, in that moment, it's like, I have to be like, no, this is great, you're doing so good. It's like—this is just taking away time that we could actually be working on the paper and making it better.

In this case, the tutor has a difficult time offering praise—another motivational scaffolding method—in the wake of negative self-talk. These tutors are taught motivational scaffolding strategies in the tutoring practicum and thus see these strategies as part of the display affect requirements of the job. Many of these strategies such as demonstrations of concern, praise, and optimism are directly referenced in the interviews when discussing surface-acting behaviors. Maintaining some degree of positivity in the face of negative affects was another area tutors reported engaging in surface acting.

Addressing political and ethical difference was another theme that emerged in surface-acting behaviors. For instance, one tutor described,

Yeah. I think, um, if the writer is writing a topic, um—I'll use an example—
there was a writer who was writing a paper about a transgender person and
kept misgendering them throughout the paper and . . . they—when I told
them, you know, this person is a woman, you need to refer to her as such,
um, the writer got rather offended and we exchanged a few words and I said,
you know, you're writing this paper for this class, your professor is going
to expect you to use the correct terms. And it was kind of snippy. It was
tense, and I had to step back a little bit because I have friends who have been
misgendered, and I know how that can affect people. And it made me fairly
angry, but you can't get in a screaming match in a session.

Here the tutor's frustration with the writer's act of misgendering created dissonance for the tutor, who felt like they had to comport themselves profession-
ally during the session. Similar stories were shared in other interviews about
topics such as depression or the "authenticity" of mental health designation
in general. That is, when writers dismissed neurodiversity or other forms of
diversity, tutors struggled with how to engage these writers.

Conversely, tutors also reported engaging in surface acting when encountering political or ethical stances with which they agreed.

S1: And I think it's so tough, too, because, like, one of my least favorite
things, actually, is when a writer comes in with, um—and this is just,
'cause me, personally, like, my personal view is, if a writer comes in with
something that I, like, fully agree with, and the, uh, evidence behind it is
not what it could be, or, like, there are kind of, like, those logical—then
it, then it, for me it gets harder, because I'm, I'm, like, oh, I want to work
with the writer on this paper to make it, like, completely flawless—but
that's not impossible, or, that's not possible, I don't think, to really, fully
like, just in a session, work through a complete paper and be like, here,
here, here, everything, like, there you go, like—and, also, that's not
even what we're supposed to do, so it's like, it gets even tougher.

S3: Yeah.

S2: And you may even have your own, like, gossip to add. Like, if you've
heard something—especially about, like, political stuff—you're, like,
you're not supposed to be giving your opinion on that sort of stuff, or
your sources might be unfounded and you might accidentally send them
down, like, a rabbit hole.

In short, tutors tended to feel that a paper that aligned too closely with their
values jeopardized their ability to act in the sort of politically neutral way they

imagined a session should be. Interestingly, during their practicum training and in staff meetings, the tutors are taught that writing, writing tutoring, and assessment are inherently political acts. This is, of course, at odds with larger narratives about the university, which imagine a normative "neutral" stance. Consequently, tutors always already feel these tensions, even (and perhaps especially) in social justice–conscious centers.

Finally, tutors reported surface-acting behaviors when working with writers on personal topics that they may have experienced or that triggered them in some way. One tutor, for example, described their experiences working with writers taking a religion course on death and dying. They explained that there had been a lot of death in their family, and that they had to maintain a positive demeanor during sessions. Often in cases like these, tutors reported compartmentalizing when dealing with personal issues or mental health struggles. Interestingly, those tutors with the least experience were the ones who reported compartmentalization or surface acting the most. According to a tutor in their first semester at the writing center with about 2 months experience at the time of their interview,

> Sometimes I feel like I have to be happy all the time, since I'm working with people, and, like, just kind of, like, working in, like, an intimate setting where you are, like, right next to a person and in—people are, like, showing you their writing, and you just, you just have to be, sometimes you just feel like you have to be happy. Sometimes you walk in and you're just like, ugh, I don't want to work, and then you step through and you're, like, put on a smile.

Whereas relatively new tutors such as this expressed a tendency to compartmentalize, more experienced tutors frequently expressed that for them surface acting was unnecessary or that compartmentalization and surface acting were more difficult for them than deep acting.

> S3: Yeah, because, like, I, like, when I—in the summer, when I work an actual customer service job, like, I was going through personal stuff, like, during that, and I was working way longer hours at that job, but it was different because the interactions were fleeting with people. Like, I would, like, take their order, give them their food, like—and it would be—we're done.
>
> S2: Mm-hmm.
>
> S3: So I didn't have to invest for—I could kind of check out, I guess, in that one. Like, I didn't have to invest personally—
>
> S1: Yeah.

> S3:—in that interaction with people, even though I was interacting with more people than I do in the writing center, but the writing center—because it's literally one-on-one—I'm more, like—I have to be more mindful of, like, my—how I'm being perceived, I guess.

The tutor's use of the word *investment* in terms of the relationship with their tutoring partners echoes Hobfoll et al.'s (2018) second principle of conservation of resources (CoR) theory: "People must invest resources in order to protect against resource loss, recover from losses, and gain resources" (p. 105). In short, through deep acting and emotional investment, this experienced tutor demonstrates how they budget emotional resources to sustain themselves in their emotional labor.

DEEP-ACTING BEHAVIORS

Overall, tutors reported engaging much more readily in deep-acting behaviors than in surface-acting behaviors. Deep acting—or emotional effort—requires still more sustained emotional labor in that the tutor works to actually change their affect to match the expectations of the situation. Most remarked on the importance of authenticity to themselves while acknowledging the need to adopt certain personas at work. An emblematic example of this stance can be seen in formulations such as this statement from the third interview:

> I think for the most part the emotions that I show writers are genuine. Um, sometimes when I'm having a bad day—it isn't necessarily fake, it's just, like, reminding myself that, like, my bad day isn't, like—kind of like what [S3] said a while ago. It's just like, my bad day doesn't affect this.

In another instance, in responding to a question about trying to create certain emotions in themselves as opposed to simply presenting the preferred affect, one exchange consisted of the following:

> S3: Yeah, I kind of feel the same way. I think that . . . it's easy for me to, like, turn on a certain, like, face to put on for the writing center, but I don't find that to be particularly, like, fake. I think that it feels pretty genuine. Um . . . yeah, it's just, like—part of being in the writing center makes you want to feel like you're, like, putting on a good face for everybody. Not just to put on a good face, but because it's just the . . . the feeling that the center gives off, I think.
>
> S2: I think so. 'Cause I worked, um . . . retail. And, with that, you have your fake retail persona—

S3: Yep.

S1: Yeah.

S2: Um, but I definitely, I think—well, I do try to be, you know, a bit more professional in the writing center. It doesn't feel like I have created a work persona for myself. It feels like me.

There seems to be an awareness here of contributing to an overall culture or atmosphere that encourages tutors to alter their feelings to match it. The notion of community or atmosphere were often used to describe deep-acting behaviors, which in turn were often described as coming with experience at the center. Accordingly, much of the sorts of compartmentalization described by more inexperienced tutors who engaged in surface-acting behaviors is less present in those with some experience in these interviews. In sum, emotional labor takes a variety of forms in writing center practice. However, perhaps just as interesting as these expressions of emotional effort and dissonance are how tutors perceive the "preferred affect" of the writing center.

EXPERIENCE AND ITS RELATIONSHIP TO EMOTIONAL EFFORT AND DISSONANCE

Much of the emotional dissonance experienced by tutors was in enacting motivational scaffolding strategies, in displaying empathy, in maintaining a politically neutral stance during sessions, and in maintaining a positive or neutral affect in response to negative affects demonstrated by their peers or when encountering deeply personal or triggering writing. This is not to say that they felt these behaviors were always at odds with their feelings but rather that this dissonance was most likely to occur in these activities. This dissonance, however, was mostly described by the more inexperienced tutors in the focus groups. More experienced tutors, in contrast, tended to report behaviors that mapped more to deep acting, expending emotional effort to change their internal feelings.

On the one hand, this difference might be explained in terms of the randomness of those in the focus groups: A total of 11 interview respondents is not likely representative of the nearly 50 member staff. Generalizing beyond that to writing center tutors more broadly is also obviously not methodologically feasible. On the other hand, this finding is confirmed by work done examining crossover models of affective resource management. Bolger et al. (1989) defined crossover as an interpersonal process wherein the stress experienced by one person affects others in the environment. Conversely, self-efficacy and engagement can also cross over, contributing to members more steeped in the organization to having greater reserves of those emotions (Waugh & Fredrickson, 2006; Westman, 2001).

This difference may also indicate that experience assists tutors in more aptly perceiving the emotion requirements of the position and thus doing away with unnecessary surface-acting behaviors; as I will explain below, experience and training in writing center work requires a great deal of emotional intelligence. As Lee and Ok (2012) determined, "EI is positively associated with EE and . . . EI is negatively associated with ED" (p. 1108). In other words, those with higher levels of emotional intelligence are more likely to expend effort to change their feelings to match the requirements of the situation rather than simply changing their affect and masking their true feelings. I intuit that, due to the emotionally intensive nature of the work, experienced tutors have more time to develop their emotional intelligence.

However, it may also indicate that more experienced tutors and those more inclined to engage in emotional effort have been successfully interpellated as ideological subjects into the value system of the writing center: on the one hand, a liberatory space seeking to enact social justice–oriented pedagogies attuned to the needs and desires of the writers who seek it out; on the other hand, an instrument in the larger neoliberal and colonialist projects of the university wherein linguistic and cultural difference is smoothed over in favor of better *writers* rather than better *writing*. Consequently, veteran tutors internalize these paradoxes, leading to, as I argue below, a form of alienation from their labor that manifests both as guilt and its converse in cynicism.

BURNOUT: EMOTIONAL EXHAUSTION, DEPERSONALIZATION, AND REDUCED PERSONAL SATISFACTION

The focus group testimonies attest to the fact that burnout is often the result of larger ebbs and flows in the emotional rhythm of a semester rather than as the result of individual sessions—it is a cumulative response to the workplace overall. For instance, subjects agreed that over the course of a given semester, they were most likely to feel emotional exhaustion around midterms and finals—both as students and as writing center tutors. Tutors also felt that having too many appointments back-to-back tended to exhaust them, speaking to the inherently emotionally intensive nature of the work. Our center has traditionally had a use rate of higher than 85%, meaning that for every 10 hours scheduled, 8.5 of them are booked with either appointments or with administrative work. Consequently, during busier times of the semester it is not unusual for our tutors to have several appointments in a row.

In terms of the types of shifts that affected them most, they generally reported that shifts occurring during walk-in hours—where there are no appointments but rather writers can simply walk in—also tend to be more stressful than their appointment counterparts. Tutors claimed that this was due to not being able to expect with whom they might be working (or on what) as well as the shorter nature of the sessions themselves. The sessions at this center typically last 50 minutes, but during walk-in hours, the sessions are 25 minutes. In short, during peak traffic times in the semester (and shift), consultants expend more emotional resources and thus are more susceptible to burnout.

Subjects also reported things beyond the center affecting their emotional state at the center such as homework, due dates for projects, exams, and personal issues. What's more, the more experienced tutors reported difficulty compartmentalizing their identities, as demonstrated in exchanges such as this:

> S2: I think, uh, as my schedule heats up, like, where midterms come or when exams are coming, I definitely feel . . . stress more. Um, I think, for me, it's personal life that affects how I perform on the job more so than, um, the responsibilities of the job itself. Um, I try to be very, like, focused on work while I'm at work and if my personal life is, like, falling to pieces or, like, my academic life is falling to pieces, I definitely feel more of that at work.

> S3: Yeah, essentially the same. I think—so, obviously, doing a lot of onlines can be pretty stressful, but also, like, once November, December rolls around, I typically have a hard time with seasonal depression and that—it's often, like, really easy for me to fall into a groove of just feeling burnt out at work. Um, even though it's not related to work at all.

> S2: Yeah.

Subject 3 in that interview describes doing "onlines"—asynchronous online sessions—in this exchange. Those sessions are reserved for online courses, the schedule for which are slightly different than the standard face-to-face 16-week semester at this university. Consequently, the traffic for those sessions tends to increase at times that do not synchronize with the regular semester. In turn, tutors who have been trained to conduct onlines will experience more "peak" times than others.

Interestingly, feeling busy at work was just as often a source of stress relief for many of the tutors in the focus groups. That is, work at the center often provided them a way to focus their attention *away* from sources of stress out-side of the center. This finding affirms Simmons et al.'s (2020) findings on stress in writing center tutors, wherein "overall findings suggest that tutors' stress levels significantly decreased from pre-shift to post-shift" (p. 20). This also affirms one of Hochschild's (2012) assertions that emotional labor can be affirming and engaging.

Depersonalization among the tutors did not seem to necessarily come from stress but rather in response to depersonalizing behavior from their dyad partners. That is, when tutors felt that they were depersonalized by the writers during their shifts, depersonalization became a face-saving strategy or a way to conserve their own emotional resources in that session by mirroring the affect of their dyad partner. One tutor remarked,

> Or like when they want you essentially to write their paper. And they come in and you try having a conversation and stuff, and they just are not—they don't want to talk to you, they just want you to come in and fix it, essentially. Or, like, my professor said that this is wrong . . . go. And it's really hard to want to be like, oh, yeah, that's really frustrating, or like, I can see how that might be an issue, like, I know I struggle with this—and they just sit there like, okay, so fix it. And it's like—yeah, it's—that's what it feels like, it feels like they're rushing you. Like, okay, let's get past this point so you can just do what needs to be done. And I feel like it's really hard to even just want to not be impersonal with them, because they are essentially looking at you like you are a service, instead of as a person.

One of the indicators of depersonalization as measured by Lee and Ok (2012) is the reported sense of emotional hardening. Most of the tutors in the focus group interviews, however, commented that they did not feel a tendency to depersonalize their session partners, even when they felt stress or burnout. On the contrary, subjects felt that rather than hardening them, the job actually made them more empathetic and explicit with writers in how they respond. In the following example, for instance, the tutor explains how experience in emotionally charged sessions has taught them to navigate boundaries and how to respond empathetically and appropriately for the situation.

> And you kind of know that, but working in the writing center, you—you really experience it firsthand. Like, when someone tells you, my parents got divorced at age seven, or, like, my parents died in a car crash, or—these other things that, you, just—you have no advanced warning of. You have no idea who this person is, and then, you're just privy to these, like, intimate details

of their life. Um, I've had stu—writers write about coming out. Um, and these very, very personal topics and . . . working through that I think has better prepared me for being a teacher, for when that will happen, but, the first few times that happened at the writing center, I didn't quite know how to handle it. It was just kind of like, oh, oh you're sharing this with me. I am a stranger, um—I'm glad you trust me, but I, like, I need a minute, you know?

The tutor followed up with recent examples of sessions wherein the writer discussed highly personal issues. Rather than depersonalization or facile demonstrations of sympathy, the tutor described how those emotions affected the writing, how writing might help the writer process those emotions, and how writing might have changed the writer's perception of those issues.

Finally, most reported that despite occasional feelings of burnout, overall they were satisfied with the job and felt accomplished in achieving it. Feelings of personal accomplishment tended to be represented by the ability to motivate writers or get them to revise expectations about the center or the session; of realizing that their expertise lies in scaffolding writers' ability to write rather than knowing everything about writing; in being empathetic; in receiving recognition from their tutoring partners; and in seeing how what they've learned in the writing center may apply to other areas in their lives. In short, their sense of accomplishment was often itself dependent on a display of emotion or in their skills' relevance to other aspects of their lives.

Guilt

As described by Ben-ze'ev (2001), guilt is not necessarily (or exclusively) a response to a moral failure but rather a violation of certain norms. It is relational and often bound up in a perceived failure to honor the needs of others around us. Writing center practice, which often adopts normative stances regarding that practice, can thus often place tutors in a position where perceived pedagogical norms are at odds with the perceived needs of writers, where those norms are at odds with the emotional needs of the tutors, or where the perceived needs of the writers are at odds with the emotional needs of the tutors.

Consequently, two strong themes emerged in the testimony regarding guilt: the tutors' conservation of emotional resources and their positioning in the university. That is, they often felt guilt after setting boundaries or emotionally withdrawing in sessions. Similarly, they often felt guilt when they struggled to navigate some of the moral/political dilemmas inherent in writing center work, particularly when their training put them at odds with instructor feedback or expectations (and thus the needs of the writers). If burnout is composed of emotional exhaustion, depersonalization or cynicism, and reduced job satisfaction, then it makes sense that guilt—one aspect of emotional exhaustion—has been studied the most out of burnout behaviors in the writing center. After all, the tutors in this study largely avoided depersonalizing behaviors (which tend to correlate with surface-acting behaviors) and tended to be satisfied in their jobs.

Guilt's relationship to emotional exhaustion, however, is complicated. Chang (2009) designates guilt as a cause of emotional exhaustion. Her appraisal perspective on teacher burnout identified several emotions that contribute to exhaustion, and of these antecedent emotions, "guilt is a self-caused emotion, which is common for teachers who perceive they are responsible for high importance and high incongruence situations. It often involves the moral purposes embedded in teachers' professional missions" (Chang, 2009, p. 208). High importance and high incongruence situations are those that are relevant to the teacher's goals but out of accord with those goals: unruly students, poor overall grades, a lack of needed resources, and so on. In the particular case of guilt, Chang (2009) noted that guilt (as compared to anger, frustration, or anxiety) also is aroused when "events are perceived to have high control potential" (p. 206)—where the individual perceives themself to have some degree of agency in the situation.

Regarding tutoring contexts, guilt would likely arise when situations are incongruent with a tutor's goals, particularly when that tutor perceives themself to have some degree of power, control, or responsibility in those situations. Although tutors do not have as much power as teachers might, they are still often regarded as experts and authority figures, and that lack of power is often at odds with, as Chang put it, the "moral purposes embedded" in writing centers' "professional missions." Given the highly personal, one-to-one nature of the relationships in writing center sessions compared to the many-to-one nature of typical classroom teaching relationships, high levels of incongruence may be felt even more keenly by tutors.

Accordingly, much of what the interviewees said affirm Chang's (2009) findings. Much of the data also affirms Dixon's (2017) and Nicklay's (2012) findings about guilt being bound up in directiveness, as well. However, much more of the testimony complicated and troubled the idea of guilt being exclusively related to directiveness or that the tutors' goals were always in alignment with what they perceived to be the center's goals. Rather, this testimony often highlighted the choices tutors felt they had to make to conserve their own emotional resources. For example, in the following statement, the tutor explains,

> If it's a particularly long session, I can tell that, by the end of it, sometimes—it's not necessarily that, like, I have the urge to, like, skip over stuff, but like, sometimes I can feel myself not being as effective because I'm just like—I really need that fifty minutes to end so I can take, like, a brain break, and I just feel guilty that, sometimes, like, at the tail end of the session, I'm not always as helpful.

Here guilt arises in that the tutor feels they're "not as helpful" due to being emotionally fatigued. In short, this tutor and others frequently discussed guilt as a byproduct of trying to balance the needs of the writers with their own personal needs—to relax their attentiveness, to decompress emotionally after such attentiveness. Indeed, that awareness of their own emotional state and attentiveness to it demonstrates a fair degree of emotional intelligence. Still, many other reasons for guilt emerged among the testimonies offered by tutors and were affirmed across interview groups.

One of the most persistent themes in the interviews, for example, was that of the emotional labor in encountering and negotiating cultural and linguistic differences. For instance, one tutor spoke of working with a Black student on a paper for a first-year composition (FYC) course about their home dialect and the frictions the student experienced between it and the expectations of school. Somewhat ironically, the student had received feedback from the instructor to basically maintain a more academic voice. The tutor struggled with their own feelings about the instructor while trying to assist the writer in negotiating a troubled situation.

> So then they were very clearly unhappy—and I was not happy to help them with it. Or, to—I—whatever, also quote "help," but, I was, like, to work with them on it. But it wasn't, um, it was something that was really challenging solely because I had to, uh, like, maneuver around this thing that I fully agreed with, but then I had to meet with the standards of, uh, whatever this professor was thinking, even though that was something that inherently I thought was wrong. And I—it was just really tough 'cause even by the end of the session, they weren't happy, but, and—I, I tried to, like, you know, explain my meaning.

This tutor expressed a great deal of guilt in trying to work with the student to meet the professor's expectations. Though having been trained in linguistic justice and having read excerpts from *Writing Centers and the New Racism*, the tutor was placed in the unenviable position of working with a writer to match the instructor's raced view of "acceptable" academic English in an essay on the problem of that very topic. Others in the interview acknowledged the writer's and tutor's plight and made references to encountering similar situations. In instances like these, the tutor is often put in a moral dilemma: to successfully act as part of the apparatus to regulate/assimilate a literacy subject to the dominant literacy or to attempt to subvert it at the risk of further marginalizing the writer. While writing center scholars such as Grimm (2011) and Greenfield and Rowan (2011) have described strategies for navigating these fraught situations, tutors inevitably encounter situations where they feel they cannot adequately address the complicated ethical and emotional obligations needed of them. The presumably white tutor's privilege doubtless complicated the session further.

Guilt in encountering difference and privilege came up in other ways in the interviews. For instance, a tutor in another interview spoke of a growing awareness of their privilege when coming into contact with the personal writing of students more disadvantaged than they:

> S1: Um, I work a lot with students who mention . . . divorce in their assignments. Usually, I've seen a few decision analysis essays over . . . kids—or, these writers—as children, making decisions as to which parent they wanted to live with—and stuff. And that has—my parents are still together and always have been, and I'm very thankful for that. But, sometimes I feel . . . strange, like, giving them, like—

> INTERVIEWER: So, when it's like, a personal subject, you kind of feel odd talking about . . . about the paper itself.

> S1: Yeah. Yeah, 'cause I don't like, I don't really relate to that. *Or I don't really want to try* and relate to that, as much, because it's obviously a very hard thing for a person to go through. (Emphasis added)

In brief, because tutors often possess privileges their writer partners do not, reminders of such seem to induce guilt. Perhaps more striking, however, is the implicit construction of empathy in this formulation. For the tutor in this exchange, empathy is a voluntary act or a choice: "I don't really want to try and relate to that." The consultant felt guilt not necessarily (or exclusively) from encountering difference but rather from having to cordon off his own ability to relate due to its emotional toll, which is also a privilege. The decision to not try is indicative of Hobfoll's (2018) conservation of resources (CoR) theory, wherein the tutor perceives a limited resource (their emotional reserves) and chooses to conserve it to avoid burnout. Because the tutor feels some sense of agency in deploying this resource and chooses not to, he feels guilt.

Even when not speaking explicitly about guilt, tutors described such when discussing encounters with difference. One tutor discussed writers who work on papers that are both personal and politicizing:

> S4: So they're, they're—they've chosen to write about something that's pretty personal. And I think sometimes they get there just wanting help on their essay, and then they realize, like, oh wait, I'm gonna, like—now they're gonna know this about me. You know, like, and uh, and sometimes . . . it's, yeah, it's pretty difficult to address, like, someone who . . . whose, like, beliefs are, like, very, very different from yours and may be incorrect, but also, like, just addressing it as a piece of writing and not—I don't . . . you don't . . . yeah, you know what I mean? Not taking it as a personal sort of attack or . . . something that you have to take to heart, to sort of combat.

This tutor and others in the interviews struggled with guilt from either feeling as though they could not contradict the writer for fear of alienating them. Conversely, they also felt guilty over being tacitly complicit if they said nothing or were unable to sway the writer from troubling beliefs or values.

Finally, and somewhat related to all of the other points, tutor perceptions of professor expectations (real or imagined) often induced guilt in these tutors who often felt responsible for writers' performances. At times they felt guilty (as in the example above) in reading faculty feedback written to students that was hegemonic, colonialist in its linguistic assumptions, or somehow reflective of their work with that student. Other times tutors worried more abstractly, that they would be unable to address higher- or later-order concerns sufficiently to appease a professor. They also felt guilty for being unable to fully praise or validate writers for fear of misleading those writers or being blamed if the writer received a poor grade or feedback from the professor. In short, these tutors reported feeling guilty for not being able to affectively invest more in those sessions and those writers due to the figure of the professor.

Emotional Intelligence and Cynicism

The questions in the interview script asked tutors to articulate concepts relating to emotional intelligence, asking them how they mind and regulate both their emotional states and the states of others. But in their responses, they most often tended to focus more on writers than on themselves. That is, while they often shared in the interviews their own emotional responses to certain situations or when they might feel particularly emotionally exhausted or satisfied, none spoke to how they monitor their own emotions during a session or how they regulated those emotions beyond two general trends: either through matching the positive affect of their tutoring partner or setting boundaries or emotionally withdrawing in instances where the affect was negative or the situation uncomfortable.

In terms of how they monitored the emotional state of their tutoring partners, most of the subjects indicated the importance of body language. They discussed body language in terms of posture and proximity as well as discrete behaviors like writers fidgeting, sitting on their hands, rubbing their legs, hovering their fingers over the keyboards, or simply "spacing out," disengaging from any sort of affect. In addition to body language, one focus group commented upon observing what they dubbed "overexplaining" as a key indicator of anxiety in their tutoring partners. For instance, one tutor remarked,

> I find, like, overexplanation—so, if I find something in a writer's paper, they'll be like, oh, not 'I'm sorry about that,' but they try to explain how the mistake happened. And I'm like, it's okay, it happens, I know I miss commas, too. You're typing fast, I get it.

Another tutor in that focus group replied,

> I find that a lot with, like, being able to help writers who are nervous to be here, as well. Like, they'll spend 20 minutes explaining their assignment to me, and it's, like, I get it. Let's start. What do you specifically want to work on? And they'll go, yeah, and then go right back to explaining this specific paragraph in their assignment guidelines.

Body language and verbal cues thus seemed the most frequent way tutors observed the emotional state of their session partners. In short, tutors in the interviews felt prepared to anticipate and perceive the emotional state of others. They explained several strategies to regulate others' emotional states as well. For instance, many described trying to diffuse others' negative emotions through talk or disengaging. Others described taking breaks to de-escalate heated sessions or situations. Joking and redirecting toward the topic were frequent methods tutors described using to avoid what they felt were unhelpful emotions. Finally, some described what I would refer to as mediating expectations to proactively avoid encountering difficult emotions, anticipating those emotions well in advance of overt displays.

A few discussed "metatalk" about the session or "breaking the fourth wall," wherein they would acknowledge the difficulty of the situation itself with their session partner.

> S1: Like, in that, you can tell that somebody is—even though, then, they've made this appointment, that they've—and now that you're working with them, and they've realized that, then you can tell that they're, like, kind of shying away, closing—and, you know, you can try to, uh, maneuver around it and say, you know, of course this is a really, like, emotional, uh, piece of work, and like, you know, you can try to, uh, discuss with them how then you're not, like, there to assess emotional state or anything, but even to that extent, I mean, nobody is ever able to fully detach themselves—or, detach their emotions from that piece.
> [*The other subjects each agree.*]
>
> S4: And usually I feel like bringing it up, like, kind of breaking the fourth wall down or whatever, and, just . . . acknowledging that sometimes— I'm like, well, is that gonna make it worse, you know? Are they gonna be like, oh, well, now it's gonna be even more awkward.

Many tutors felt capable of perceiving and regulating emotion in others but described reluctance or hesitance to do so, often citing moral concerns about manipulating others. In one interview, for example, a tutor stated:

> S1: I think—because I, I don't want to—personally, I don't want to be somebody who, uh, like, changes others' emotional states, unless it is in regards to what can further, uh, what can further serve to, um, make their writing better or the session more successful for whatever their wants are. Um—'cause I mean, I, I feel like, you know, saying, like, you have to change your emotional state for me to be, uh, for me to be a resource for you is, like, it's a little bit, uh—it's, it's a little bit gatekeep-y.
>
> S2: Yeah.
>
> S3: Mm-hmm.
>
> S1: Um, you know. Whereas then, um, being able to say, like, I don't want you to change your emotional state, but it might be, like, easier—not, like, directly, but—
>
> S2: Right.
>
> S1:—you know trying to figure that out for yourself and maneuver around that. That's always the case that I always struggle with.

Here the tutor shows concern about imposing their own values around emotional display on their tutoring partner, worried that doing so is a form of withholding or being "gatekeep-y." Still, the consultant hedges by stating, "Unless it is in regard to what can further, uh, what can further serve to, um, *make their writing better* or the session more successful for whatever their wants are." The tutor acknowledges their ability and experience in regulating others' emotional states and willingness to do so to better align the writer with a broad conception of what good writing is in the university setting.

A tutor in another interview acknowledged their ambivalence about regulating others' emotional states in response to a question about fostering a certain atmosphere at the center. The tutor clearly valued the culture of the center, which itself is often reflective of white, middle-class values—those of the majority who work in the center and of the university as a whole.

> S3: I mean, a lot of it is just, like, modeling the sort of behavior that, like, you're looking for, hoping for, um, in others, so . . . in the center. I try to be relaxed and friendly and approachable and warm and opening.
>
> S2: Mm-hmm.
>
> S1: I try and get them to talk about themselves for at least, like, two minutes at the beginning of the session.
>
> S2: Mm-hmm.
>
> S1: Just. uh . . . again, 'cause people like to talk about themselves and I'm manipulative in a positive way.
> [*Laughter*]

The tutor acknowledges that the nature of a session is inherently bound up in affect and that prompting the writer to talk about themself is not solely about the essay but a way to establish rapport. The tutor views emotional regulation as "manipulative in a positive way." The laughter from the other subjects indicates that the comment was a joke, but a joke based on a mutual understanding of the often-implicit emotional labor inherent in the session. This response, along with the one before it and others in the interviews, make plain a certain (if necessary) cynicism that tutors must adopt regarding their emotional labor. They recognized the need for monitoring and regulating others' emotional states, and they reported a variety of surface and deep-acting behaviors to facilitate that regulation. They felt some ambivalence, however, about the ethics of doing so unless it furthered what they saw as the center's mission.

Rather than depersonalizing behavior, cynicism in these focus group interviews manifested as something else. For Sloterdijk (1987), cynicism is enlightened false consciousness, wherein the subject realizes their conditions and how these conditions are at odds with their ideals and yet finds a way to persist in these conditions. Rickert (2007) examined this notion in *Acts of Enjoyment*, problematizing the use of cultural studies in the composition classroom. Rickert (2007) considered how students, when taught ways to critique dominant ideological practices, still indulge in those practices, finding that "their adeptness led them to write competent, even excellent papers, but that was the extent of it. If there was any real change, it was in growing cynicism: 'Yeah, I know I don't need these seventy-five-dollar designer blue jeans, but . . .' [spending ensues]" (p. 2). In essence, Rickert (2007) problematized the modernist notion that simply introducing "better" discourse to students will cause those students to adopt a more enlightened, perhaps even anti-ideological, position. To extend this conception to the tutors, they are informed about colonialist and white supremacist practices in the university as well as techniques to monitor and regulate emotional states. They are given tools to address the situation they are in, but that situation doesn't really seem to change, and thus tutors must adapt. Sometimes it's a matter of conserving their own emotional resources; other times it is bound up in overtly using surface- or deep-acting behaviors to motivationally scaffold their tutoring partner; and still other times, it comes from trying to reconcile their own politics and privilege in the situation they find themselves, whether that situation is helping a student navigate white supremacy in instructor expectations or facilitating a session with a student experience class-based hardships that they haven't.

The tutors in this study have been trained in social justice–oriented pedagogies; they work in a writing center with a fairly explicit social justice mission; they can speak fluently about the importance of linguistic and dialect diversity. However, as many of the prior excerpts from focus interviews demonstrate, they often display a certain ambivalence about these values in their practice, acknowledging their situatedness in an affective exchange where those values are not necessarily shared by other stakeholders involved in that exchange: their session partner, the professor, or even the institution writ large. In brief, they must accommodate the values that they negotiate from their training to the reality of their practice. Similarly, the tutors have learned approaches to help monitor and regulate their session partner's emotional state during the session, which is often bound up in negotiating issues of linguistic diversity and the conservation of their own emotional resources. Accordingly, two unlikely affects are bound together as a form of alienation from their labor. On the one hand, the forms of cynicism I've relayed above could be seen as a form of depersonalization—particularly when the tutors feel they must withdraw emotionally from the situation or individual. On the other hand, their reported feelings of guilt around these same actions seem to indicate that the two are intertwined. Writing center administrators (WCAs) must thus be mindful of how these feelings intersect, are fostered, and contribute to burnout.

Conclusion and Takeaways: Using Managerial Strategies to Combat Burnout

Although I spend more time in the next chapter discussing training for emotional intelligence, affect, and the body, here I wish to consider some takeaways for other directors and researchers. Perhaps most encouragingly, the tutors in these focus groups report handling their stress well and have developed assorted strategies for navigating potentially stressful sessions. Experience in the writing center also seems to help tutors develop deep-acting behaviors that correlate with a high emotional quotient (EQ) and thus less likelihood of burning out (Lee & Ok, 2012). They also reported high job satisfaction and personal accomplishment: for these tutors, writing center work is meaningful work.

Like other researchers, I see the main issues involved with burnout to be bound up in management. I wish here to heed and extend Giaimo's (2023) call to begin considering our work in managerial terms, because "in not framing our work within managerial contexts . . . it is easy to fall into unintentional behaviors that mimic the work habits of late-stage capitalism" (p. 115). And like Giaimo (2023), my research into burnout is preliminary but asks us to consider our positioning in our institutional contexts and how that might inform our approach to management. Perhaps ironically, then, research in the fields of workplace psychology, human resources, and management has generated a great deal of knowledge about emotional labor's relationship to phenomena such as deep and surface acting, burnout, workplace relations, and more. If we wish to sustain the sorts of activism, social justice, and similar forms of writing center pedagogy, I believe embedding such research in our practice has a lot to offer.

For instance, the testimonies point to other managerial practices that can help address and ameliorate burnout. Scheduling and the timing of sessions obviously played a big role in those feelings among tutors. Our associate director (AD) and I have developed ways to help tutors adjust their schedules at more stressful points in the semester such as midterms and the weeks leading up to finals week. We have also adopted policies about the 10 minutes between our 50-minute sessions as being sacrosanct times for consultants to decompress. Attention, like other cognitive and emotional resources, is limited and rhythmic. Such regular breaks allow for that resource to be replenished. These breaks can help stave off the assorted negative feelings such as frustration, boredom, and other emotions associated with burnout. We can also build in breaks from appointments in our scheduling by switching up the sorts of tasks we ask of our consultants. We might pull a consultant off the schedule after several appointments for some light administrative task that won't take the entirety of an hour. They might instead take on relatively easy cognitive or affective tasks like staffing the front desk that, again, will provide them with more downtime.

The present study affirms the findings of the hospitality management study that inspired it (Lee & Ok, 2012), but it also differs in a few substantive ways. Therefore, I share Lee and Ok's (2012) recommendations for management to consider how they might be adapted for writing center contexts. More crucially, however, I explain where those implications are insufficient—or even dangerous—for our contexts. I will then address these issues in the following chapter on training for emotional literacy.

One of Lee and Ok's (2012) recommendations is to promote deep-acting behaviors—emotional effort—in workers' service encounters, given the dysfunctional effects of emotional dissonance on job satisfaction. In the present study, the more experienced tutors described behaviors conforming to deep acting and to high degrees of emotional intelligence and job satisfaction. Conversely, more inexperienced tutors tended to rely on surface acting, which, as Lee and Ok (2012) found, tends to correlate with depersonalization and emotional exhaustion. This is not to say that surface acting is inherently bad. As Hochschild (2012) herself pointed out, "We are commonly aware of pretending to feel something when we want to be polite. Pretending is a statement of deference to the other, an offering" (p. 82). Surface acting is thus a part of care, an offering. Being explicit about emotional labor—acting to produce affects—as an act of care with our staff may make them less skeptical or cynical about their own work to regulate others' emotions. Based on the research, however, I believe it is in our tutors' best interest to help them make the transition from surface acting to deep acting in the demonstration of that care. Implementing instruments such as the SPAFF in staff training can help address this recommendation through "teach[ing] employees appropriate emotional display techniques or necessary skills" (Lee & Ok, 2012, p. 1110). The question of what constitutes "appropriate emotional display" will be taken up momentarily once I have had an opportunity to address the other recommendations, and it will be addressed more fully in the next chapter. That said, it's clear from the testimony that tutors are already developing and using display techniques and skills inherent to EI in their sessions: whether through "metatalk" or identifying nervousness in their dyad partner to adjust their strategies. A more deliberate approach to deep acting will likely help them extend and refine these skills. I also believe that using the SPAFF to help them self-monitor and regulate may be crucial in successful deep-acting behaviors.

Second, Lee and Ok (2012) urged hospitality organizations to work with employees to recharge emotional resources: "For employees to keep their emotional resources charged, management should listen to their employees, particularly when they have concerns about work, and encourage employees and managers to share experiences and skills with each other" (p. 1110). Many of the tutors reported their own dissonance, guilt, and cynicism arising from feeling a lack of emotional resources to address the task at hand, so this seems especially relevant to writing center contexts. Staff meetings, conversation hours, and other professional development opportunities could provide tutors paid time to commiserate and for WCAs to listen and consider their perspectives. I would also encourage WCAs to develop means for their employees to provide anonymous feedback during the work year, and to conduct or collect exit interviews from their outgoing tutors.

Third, Lee and Ok (2012) encouraged organizations to help their "employees feel a sense of accomplishment and emotional efficacy when they perform successful EE behavior or exert EI in service encounters" (1110). For example, pre-COVID (and we're still working to reincorporate this practice once more), our center used to keep an "anonymous compliments" box wherein tutors would say nice things about what they've observed in others' practice. These compliments would be shared at staff meetings. In addition to helping boost our tutors' confidence and sense of accomplishment, these public acts of praise also make explicit our community's values, norms, and mission. Consequently, tutors may thus be more inclined toward deep acting, knowing that their own values are more in alignment with the situation at hand than they might if such norms remained implicit. Accordingly, a writing center's mission statement, philosophy statements, and statements around inclusion, diversity, and equity can and should be regularly revisited with the staff. Such review would not only make the workplace more democratic and inclusive but also serve to encourage emotional effort and investment.

Finally—and problematically—Lee and Ok (2012) explained that hospitality organizations may wish to consider using some measure of emotional intelligence in hiring and personnel decisions and to implement or develop training programs to foster employees' emotional intelligence. This makes some intuitive sense. After all, if EI correlates to emotional effort and negatively to emotional dissonance (and to a decline in the quality of service), and if emotional dissonance correlates to burnout, it makes sense that writing center directors (WCDs) would want to cultivate emotional intelligence to help tutors avoid it. Indeed, as I will explain in the following chapter, fostering emotional intelligence in tutors has been of interest to writing center studies for some time now.

However, like other measures of human ability, emotional intelligence is not an objective measurement but rather a human construct developed in historically and materially bound contexts. As I will discuss next chapter, the construct of emotional intelligence—although important and useful—was developed in the context of white supremacy, and it can often reflect values around the body based in a white and middle-classed habitus. Thus, to screen for EI may in fact simply reward those who naturally occupy that habitus and exclude those who do not. Further, as I argue in the next chapter, training for EI in writing center contexts should be informed by intersectionality and rooted in the forms of wellness developed by BIPOC scholars and activists, located in larger liberation movements. To do otherwise is to co-opt the work of these movements and perpetuate many of the injustices that can lead to burnout.

4

Training Tutors for Emotional Literacy

Reviewing the results of the focus group interviews in the previous chapter, I found that even without training, tutors were developing emotional monitoring and regulation strategies without training or scaffolding. Whether or not these were entirely successful or helpful for these tutors or their writers still isn't entirely clear to me. What is now clear to me, however, is the necessity of deliberate and purposeful training. And I believe such training requires that we reconsider concepts such as emotional intelligence. In this chapter, I work to tie such training to genre.

In a review of Mackiewicz and Thompson's *Talk About Writing* (2018), Lerner (2019) observed an implication in the book "that writing center pedagogy is a patterned genre, replicable and researchable across multiple sites and with multiple participants" (p. 463). Throughout this book (and most especially in this chapter), I move from implication to explicit argument: The peer tutoring session *is* a patterned genre. Instead of reimagining every encounter with a student writer anew, tutors follow patterns of discourse that have stabilized around the recurring rhetorical situation that is the writing center session. I argue for writing center practitioners to reenvision the writing center session as what Bakhtin (1986) would call a secondary genre. Whereas primary speech genres are "relatively stable types" (Bakhtin, 1986, p. 60) of utterances,

https://doi.org/10.7330/9781646428649.c004

secondary speech genres "absorb and digest various primary (simple) genres" (Bakhtin, 1986, p. 62). As a secondary genre, facilitating a writing center session thus adopts, appropriates, and remediates several primary genres to facilitate the desired social action in response to its rhetorical situation. That is, a tutor will use a variety of primary speech genres such as apologies, greetings, and more within the patterned discourse of the secondary genre that is the peer tutoring session. Affect, emotion, and the body writ large are features in that genre; they facilitate (and frustrate) the conveyance of meaning in larger patterns of discourse. I believe this reenvisioning of the session as a genre is crucial because it allows us to move away from problematic conceptions of emotional intelligence to instead adopt a more literacy-focused approach to emotion and affect. As I will argue, such a move is especially crucial if we want to enact a more social justice–oriented stance.

Reconsidering Emotional Intelligence

Originally coined in 1964 by Michael Beldoch, the concept of emotional intelligence (EI) was popularized in 1995 by Daniel Goleman in *Emotional Intelligence*. Although the concept of EI has several models and definitions that are contested by psychologists, in this chapter I focus on Goleman's (1995) mixed model as it is both the most well-known and the one that has gained the most traction in writing center studies. Goleman's (1995) interest lies primarily in emotional intelligence's relationship to leadership performance and the competencies and skills that drive it. Five qualities or constructs compose emotional intelligence according to Goleman (1995): self-awareness, self-regulation, social skill, empathy, and motivation (p. 37). For Goleman, these constructs in turn consist of several discrete habits of mind to cultivate these skills. For my argument here, I focus most especially on his formulation of self-regulation.

EI has been embraced by writing center studies, with numerous examinations considering the concept and exploring ways to foster emotional intelligence in tutors. Perhaps the earliest of these is Lape's (2008) *WLN* article "Training Tutors in Emotional Intelligence: Toward a Pedagogy of Empathy." In it, Lape (2008) analyzed the construction of emotions in assorted tutor training manuals and found that when they do speak of emotion, "some tutor training manuals employ a rhetoric that may place new tutors in a defensive position—on alert, waiting for the inevitable problem person to arrive" (p. 2). To address this, she drew on emotional intelligence, service learning, and other areas to argue for training that promotes empathy. Similar approaches have adopted in the literature elsewhere such as in Mattingly et al. (2021), which drew more on Edgar Schein's (2017) work to consider the ways in which group members' EI affects organizational culture in a writing center. Driscoll and Wells (2020) advocated developing emotional intelligence in tutors, comparing writing center work to care work in other professions and pointing to literature in those fields to demonstrate EI's importance. Luke Iantorno (2022) used survey data to examine "if the expenditure of emotional labor influenced the quality of work, overall job satisfaction, perceptions of co-workers and clientele, and development of emotional intelligence" (p. 204), finding that his participants wanted further training and professional development related to emotional intelligence. In brief, there is a clear exigence for exploring and cultivating emotional intelligence in writing center settings. Training in emotional intelligence has been shown to improve empathy and adaptability, and such training is crucial for successful and ethical practice in the care professions (Ilievová et al., 2013; Nightingale et al., 2018; Penprase et al., 2015). In writing center contexts, Driscoll and Wells (2020) have extended Driscoll and Powell's (2016) work identifying metacognitive emotional management skills among successful writers. They find that students who engage in "metacognitive monitoring" (n.p.)—mindfully observing their own emotions—tend to benefit from long-term transfer and learning gains. Driscoll and Wells (2020) thus argued for tutors modeling those successful emotional management skills for student writers.

Of the current body of writing center research related to emotional intelligence, Rachel Peterson's (2023) work is most like my own in this chapter in that she considered the relationship between training for emotional intelligence, equity, and fostering empathy in tutors for underrepresented groups. Peterson (2023) emphasized the need to pair training for emotional intelligence with linguistic inclusivity so that tutors are mindful of the identities producing the writing. In this chapter, I extend her argument by asserting that it may be *dangerous* to train for emotional intelligence without centering such training in linguistic and social justice.

Like many others in writing center studies, I assert and reaffirm the importance of training tutors for emotional intelligence. We *need* to be as emotionally aware and fluent as possible. However, as I argue in this chapter, training for EI is not without its problems. Researchers have shared numerous criticisms of the construct of emotional intelligence, whether that be its overstated importance in the popular literature (Landy, 2005; Mayer, 2001), the lack of clarity or precision around correlating EI and leadership qualities (Harms &

Credé, 2010; Murensky, 2000), the disconnect between knowing emotionally intelligent behaviors and behaviors themselves (Brody, 2004), and its potential conflation with conformity (Roberts et al., 2001), among others. Here I focus on two critiques. I first consider what some psychologists have referred to as the "dark side" of EI: its relationship to manipulative behaviors. Second, I discuss the concept's historical development and connections to white habitus and social norms—that is, I argue that the traits composing Goleman's constructs for EIs are in many ways a reification (and normalization) of white habitus and middle-class values.

After sharing these critiques, I work to resituate EI as emotional literacy. I argue that one way to address the concerns I raise is to reconceive the peer tutoring session as an embodied rhetorical genre, approaching training for that genre in the modes of emotional literacy and ideological genre critique. I then share some anecdotes about trainings I've facilitated to illustrate how WCDs might incorporate the SPAFF, emotional literacy, and genre theory to ethically train tutors for EI. I have three goals in mind for such training. First, I hope that such a literacy will help them become more proficient rhetors in that genre in general; fluency in emotion will make them better at facilitating sessions. Second, I think such training can attune tutors to cues in their session partners to better attend to the nuances of power and bias that intersect in that genre. Third, I hope they will become more in touch with their own emotions and better able to thus address those same issues.

THE DARK SIDE OF EMOTIONAL INTELLIGENCE

Despite the many benefits of emotional intelligence, researchers have shown that individuals can use social ability and emotional intelligence to override others' perceptions or to advance their own goals at the expense of others (Austin et al., 2014; Chamorro-Premuzic & Yearsley, 2017; Côté et al., 2011; Kilduff et al., 2010; Nozaki & Koyasu, 2013). Even in earlier studies on EI, researchers warned of its negative potential, with Mayer (2001) cautioning that "some emotionally intelligent people may manage their feelings in . . . negative ways: to manipulate, control, and exploit themselves and others" (p. 423). Similarly, Kilduff et al. (2010) considered how abilities associated with EI can be employed in competitive organizations and environments to better employ what they refer to as "dark-side tactics," including such behaviors as focusing on strategically important tactics or individuals in the organization, disguising and expressing emotion for personal gain, stirring others' emotions through misattribution, and strategically controlling emotion-laden information

(p. 133). Grieve et al. (2019) found gender roles to be an especially important consideration in emotional intelligence, explaining that "for both males and females, masculine gender roles positively predicted emotional manipulation" (p. 157).

These observations are affirmed in Nozaki and Koyasu's (2013) study, which found that those who demonstrate high interpersonal (as opposed to *intrapersonal*) EI tend to "attempt to regulate others' emotions based on their own goals" (p. 6). Nozaki and Koyasu (2013) found that EI is not an inherently prosocial or positive trait. Rather, it can facilitate the achievement of individual goals—sometimes at others' expense. Finally, psychologists Nagler et al. (2014) have examined whether socio-emotional intelligence was associated with emotional manipulation when used by personality types associated with the "dark triad" of narcissism, Machiavellianism, and psychopathy, finding that their "results further support the notion that EI can have a maladaptive aspect in interpersonal relations" (p. 50).

In short, without some attention paid to prosocial outcomes, training in emotional intelligence may backfire. As evident in the focus groups from the previous chapter, tutors tend to learn to monitor and address the emotional state of their dyad partners. Much of their self-reported guilt (and attendant cynicism) seemed to originate from when they privileged their own emotional needs (especially the conservation of their emotional resources) over what they perceived as the needs of their session partner. We may also see situations such as that in the introductory anecdotes at the beginning of that chapter: tutors may use what they develop to avoid working with writers who are inconvenient for them, even as that avoidance harms those writers—particularly minority student writers. As I explain in the next section, I worry this can be especially complicated in that the development of the construct of emotional intelligence is rooted in a racialized and classed habitus. Tutors may, such as in the case of the second anecdote, employ their EI and racial or status privilege to conserve their own resources at the expense of vulnerable populations. They may normalize certain ways of being in the world and thus marginalize others. Their expectations of "appropriate" affective displays may be hardened and reflect the preferences of a majority (white, able, heterosexual, cisgender, male), thus bringing an implicit politics of respectability to encounters with difference in the center.

THE GENEALOGY OF THE EMOTIONAL INTELLIGENCE CONSTRUCT

Americanist Michael Staub (2016) has traced the history of EI as a concept and asserts that it "cannot be told apart from a history of race and class in the

United States—and this has everything to do with one further dimension of EI and that is the significance of the ideal of self-control" (p. 60). Regulating emotion is central to emotional intelligence, and self-control is interesting in that it is hard to even consider the concept without drawing on cultural configurations of it such as the "Protestant work ethic," or "Midwestern reserve." Value statements are thus inherent in some aspects of the ostensibly measurable figure we wish to train for.

Staub (2016) pointed out that Goleman was the first to emphasize self-control in emotional intelligence, observing that earlier proponents of EI such as Salovey and Mayer (1990) conceived of EI as a much more diffuse set of skills (p. 60). Staub (2016) examined several passages in *Emotional Intelligence* demonstrating Goleman's (1995) focus on the primacy of self-control. Staub (2016) argued that in making self-control such a key part of EI, Goleman (1995) relied on Walter Mischel's (1974) experiments on delayed gratification that have since become popularly known as the "marshmallow test." In short, Mischel (1974) would offer a child a choice on a reward now or waiting a period for a greater reward: a marshmallow now or several later. Mischel (1974) reported that children who choose to delay gratification were more likely to demonstrate socially responsible behaviors and conversely less likely to demonstrate delinquent behaviors. According to Staub (2016), Goleman became convinced that this quality of delaying gratification could be acquired. In turn, Goleman's notion that self-control is an acquired skill linked to EI has since influenced Mischel.

Staub (2016) noted, however, that social psychology has a long and ideologically complicated history with the concept of self-control. In particular, he found that Mischel (1974) began to moralize the meanings of delayed gratification. Staub (2016) contextualized the development of Mischel's (1974) arguments on self-control by tracing the parallel developments in policy and research surrounding poverty, race, and class in America during the late 1960s and early 1970s. Staub (2016) found in the literature of the time that

> A circular argument emerged; people who lacked an ability to resist immediate satisfactions were more likely to fail in socioeconomic terms, while lower-class persons suffered from an inability to defer gratification. It was, as historian Alice O'Connor has noted, a "profile of lower-class personality disorders" that was "contradictory, culturally biased, and remarkably simplistic at times" and that yet continued to gain ground—at least among illiberal social policy researchers. (p. 70)

The notion that a person's individual choices and inability to control their impulses predicted their later success—despite research showing otherwise—continued to dominate the national conversation. It was this in context in 1974 that Mischel found that the "middle and upper (in contrast to lower) socioeconomic classes" demonstrated "higher intelligence, more mature cognitive development, and greater capacity for sustained attention (p. 250)." Citing that specific passage, later researchers (Wilson & Herrnstein, 1985) went on to connect delayed gratification behaviors to family settings. This, in turn, fed into racist tropes about broken homes and people of color.

As Staub (2016) explained, "The idea that familial breakdown led to deficiencies in self-control that, in turn, produced criminal behavior was not the viewpoint Mischel meant to promote, but his ideas proved very usable to an unabashedly right-wing causational theory" (p. 72). That theory permeated later research and writing connecting IQ, social mobility, and self-control, most notoriously in publications such as Herrnstein and Murray's (1994) *The Bell Curve* as well as Gottfredson and Hirschi's (1990) *A General Theory of Crime*, both of which advocated a racist, social Darwinist view of social class as meritocratic and/or self-inflicted. Staub (2016) concluded,

> The very concept of self-control had once been a profoundly racialized one. The way that coded, *now-you-see-it-now-you-don't* references to race have moved in and out of focus in the literature on self-control reveals much about the ideological work done by any social psychological theory that directs attention away from broader contexts and toward the individual's success or failure at self-management. (p. 77, emphasis his)

In short, the development of EI is traceable as a reaction to—but *also an extension of*—previous attempts to classify and measure individuals by IQ and to erase race and class from burgeoning literature on self-improvement.

Staub (2016) isn't the only writer to observe links between contemporary conceptions of EI and white supremacy. Boyd (2021), for instance, examined how EI is used

> as a filter of racial awareness by Black students and faculty in an attempt to hide their Blackness and all aspects of Black culture as not to offend or disrupt WSC [White Supremacy Culture] in higher education as a means of survival at PWIs [Predominantly White Institutions]. (p. 53)

Boyd (2021) was interested in the ways that Black students in these contexts utilize EI to meet the expectations of their white peers. EI, while invaluable for these students' self-preservation in PWIs, thus also helps normalize white racial habitus. Similarly, in an examination of Ohio's K–12 educational social and emotional learning (SEL) standards, Clark et al. (2022) found that "by ignoring racism, ableism, and other oppressions; privileging civility over productive conflict; and focusing on behaviors over emotions, especially when expressed by Black, Brown, dis/abled, and queer people, SEL standards may undermine or erase the critically productive role that emotions have played in movements for social justice" (p. 131). These values—such as "privileging civility over productive conflict"—thus enact a discourse around emotion and self-regulation that maintains racial, gendered, and abled status quos.

Values and attitudes around conceptions of emotional intelligence—especially self-control—are thus culturally coded, normalizing certain valences and ways of being in the world through the body and feeling. The code of self-regulation and the very construct of emotional intelligence are not objective or natural. Rather, they are just that—constructs developed in a certain time and place, socially and historically contingent, and predicated on the language available and the power dynamics inherent in the situation that lead to their articulation. Put another way, emotional intelligence and its subtrait of self-control are measures that may be reliable, but caution is needed in considering their validity. That is, tests of emotional intelligence can predictably produce the same results with repeat testing. But to confuse what is actually being tested—a subject's ability to respond to a given test with the preferred answers that map to the construct—with an objective measurement of an individual's self-control is to misunderstand the instrument's validity.

Consequently, I worry that to train tutors for EI, we may be implicitly (if unintentionally) imposing and normalizing a white racial habitus on them. This is already a concern in writing center studies as articulated by several scholars. For example, Haltiwanger Morrison and Nanton (2019) found that people of color often have to navigate the assumed white and middle-class habitus of writing center spaces. Similarly, Faison and Treviño (2017) located discord between the writing center's ostensibly inclusive and counter-institutional ethos and its actual practices, especially as experienced by people—and most especially women—of color. This is all to say that an uncritical approach to training for emotional intelligence may do more harm than good. As Genie Giaimo (2023) explained, "In rushing to create harmonious spaces, informed by white, middle-class aesthetics and politics, we risk speaking over and negating the voices of writing center workers that come from other backgrounds" (p. 126). I would extend this to say that the very way tutor training tends to treat affect and the "outward display" reifies white habitus and politics and thus subtly negates other voices. Given, too, that psychologists have found that EI can be deployed against marginalized others (Nozaki & Koyasu, 2013), I believe that EI cannot be taught or trained for as an apolitical instrument.

Emotional Literacy and Genre

Rather than simply ignore the issues inherent in training for emotional intelligence or elide the question altogether, I wonder if the issue can be generatively reframed. The term *emotional intelligence* is at base a metaphor used to define and explain the ability to monitor and regulate emotions. That is, the concept of IQ is drawn on as a stand-in for fluency in emotions. Just as we might be verbally or numerically intelligent, we might also have the same wherewithal regarding emotions. Early advocates of the concept were deliberate in this choice. As Staub (2016) explained, researchers

> who championed the centrality of noncognitive skills were posing a direct challenge not only to experts across the political spectrum who believed in the value of IQ as a metric. They were—and quite significantly—challenging right-wing (and often explicitly racialized) theories that stated how traditional IQ testing represented the most accurate predictor of a person's capacity for achievement. (p. 59)

It is somewhat ironic, then, that many of the characteristics these advocates were trying to explain as inherent to emotional intelligence were co-opted for other white supremacist projects. EI (which has sometimes been referred to as "EQ" as an emotional analogue for IQ) was so named to define and understand populations beyond the reductionist way that IQ was being applied at the time.

However, there are other ways to describe fluency in affect and emotion. I find an alternative metaphor for emotional intelligence—*emotional literacy*—to be especially promising for writing center purposes. Educators in the UK have come to favor *emotional literacy* as a term over emotional intelligence due to the idea that intelligence is perceived to be a measurable individual trait whereas emotional literacy is a social trait that is difficult—if not impossible—to quantify. As Alemdar and Anilan (2022) explained,

> The term "intelligence" accrues a negative connotation that would undermine the positive message (Sharp, 2001) and it tends to suggest a capacity that is innate and fixed, not teachable (Ripley & Simpson, 2007; Weare & Gray, 2003). The term "literacy," on the other hand, is more related to language and

the culture that can be improved by the use of language (Matthews, 2006). Emotional intelligence is the personal capability to understand and manage emotional information, while emotional literacy is to make use of relationships with others to better understand and process emotional information (Haddon et al., 2005). (p. 30)

Emotional literacy locates emotion in the social and thus the rhetorical. As such, this metaphor can provide a frame for rhetoricians to revisit theories around literacy and discourse and apply them to training for emotion and affect. What's more, once emotional intelligence is denaturalized and reconceived as a form of literacy, we can make its social and political dimensions more visible and available to critique and action. I believe emotional literacy can help us see the writing center session as a genre—one in which affective displays are a key feature.

Although I have argued in the introduction that facilitating a peer tutoring session is a genre, I would like to elaborate here. It is a regularly occurring rhetorical situation in which certain norms and features have coalesced into recognizable characteristics. We typically expect, for example, greetings at the beginning of the session perhaps accompanied with small talk. Then an agenda is negotiated and information about the task is gathered and shared. Depending on the particular tasks and needs of the stakeholders, a variety of discursive moves are made: questions, scaffolding, direct instruction, reader response, and still more. As the session draws to a close, tutors will typically review the session, complete a form, and consider revision plans with the writer before wrapping up and socializing at the end.

In Bakhtinian (1986) terms, the session is a secondary genre intended to facilitate an intervention in and possible reconsideration of a writer's work, inflected differently than that of, say, the teacher conference or an editor's intervention. In turn, the consultant draws on several primary speech genres. They are also inflected by their modalities—the way one raises or lowers their voice, the proximity with which they sit next to their conversation partner, body language, the manner of dress, facial expressions, and so on. As Chapter 2 demonstrated, these features often coincide with, facilitate, respond to, and/ or anticipate other rhetorical moves standard to the genre. Affective displays are, in short, features of the genre.

Accordingly, I think a genre perspective has a lot to offer for tutor training. In fact, I would argue that any time we teach consultants how to *be* in a session, we are teaching them a genre—implicitly or otherwise. This too can be dangerous because an implicit approach to teaching genre can often unwittingly adopt a prescriptive stance—wherein certain features are assumed to be *normal* or required. Consequently, we may train to what we perceive to be the conventions, which often assume a white, American, cisgender, neurotypical, able habitus. As Freedman (1994) has argued, even explicit teaching of a genre "can be dangerous" in some instances, including when students overgeneralize or focus overmuch on the form (p. 206). When we tell tutors to sit beside the writer, to maintain eye contact, to lean forward, and offer them similarly prescriptive advice without encouraging them to ask why or under what circumstances, we also prescribe certain bodies and ways of being in the world through those bodies.

For the rest of this chapter I consider examples of what a genre-based approach to tutor training might look like regarding emotional literacy. In particular, I find what Amy Devitt calls genre critique a suitable approach for this endeavor: "Rather than teaching students particular genres or strategies for learning new genres, genre critique teaches students to think critically about existing genres and their cultures" (2014, p. 154). In the case of the writing center session, rather than solely teaching new consultants the "form" of the writing center consulting genre or how to learn new genres including that one (though I acknowledge that these are important components of the process), a genre critique approach asks us to consider the ideologies enacted in the center session. What sorts of bodies are authorized to speak? In what ways are certain bodies regulated whereas others are less subject to scrutiny? Who gets to *feel* in the center?

The SPAFF can provide a framework to label features in the genre and make them available not only for use but for critique. For instance, a prescriptive way to apply the SPAFF in training would consist of encouraging tutors to make sure to employ Affection and Enthusiasm indicators early in the session (e.g., "I'm really excited for your project!" or "Let's get started"), Interest and Validation indicators throughout (e.g., backchanneling, paraphrasing, and clarification-seeking), and end the session with still more Affection and Enthusiasm indicators. Such a prescriptive approach would likely advise against displaying so-called negative affects such as Anger, Domineering, or Sadness. This paradigm, however, divorces the visible traces of rhetoric inherent in the situation from the particulars of that situation, imagining it to be universal. If we instead identify those features, "genre pedagogy also makes more visible the values and worldviews embodied in those texts" (Feez, 2002, p. 57). Although affect and emotion are only some of the features of the genre of peer tutoring, I would argue that they are some of the least understood and articulated.

Putting Theory into Practice

Here I offer a few instances of training sessions in hopes that others may adapt elements of them for their purposes. The first of these consist of our center's first "roll out" of our adaptation of the SPAFF, and the second relates to a workshop on embodiment I've offered in several contexts. While the first deals specifically with the SPAFF, the second shows how elements of the SPAFF can be used to help interrogate seemingly normalized affective displays that are deeply rooted in race- and sex-based privilege. Both instances demonstrate how a genre pedagogy approach can be adopted for encouraging tutors to consider the political dimensions of affect and emotion in their sessions.

LEARNING THE SPAFF

Once our coding team had adapted the SPAFF for more writing center–specific purposes, we devoted a staff meeting to sharing and discussing it. The beginning of the meeting was spent summarizing the assorted affect codes and how we adapted them. We asked our staff to consider situations in which they might encounter (or have encountered) those affective displays. For example, tutors shared experiences of Defensiveness, recalling times when writers would change the subject once tutors identified deeper issues in an essay. Some talked about feeling Disgust while encountering graphic descriptions in medical writing and having to be mindful of their affect with their session partner. Even as we simply reviewed the codes, several tutors observed that many of the indicators failed to consider neurodivergence and context on their own. For instance, several remarked that while "Incessant Speech" is an indicator of Domineering, it may in fact not be related to that sort of behavior but may instead indicate neurodivergence or nervousness.

Once the staff reviewed the codes, they were broken into small groups to discuss two general questions:

- What affects do you believe would be the most common in a writing center session and why?
- Which ones do you think are the most important to know and why?

After spending time in small groups, we reconnected as a full staff to share our responses and continue the discussion. I chose these two questions to pose because I felt they not only were broad enough to get our staff to consider affect in a variety of ways but also would start identifying those affective cues as features of the genre. That is, by asking them to consider what they suspected would be the most common cues, I was asking them to review their prior experiences with affect to determine the relationship between common tutoring "moves" in the genre and the affects they anticipate, produce, and/or facilitate. By asking them which they felt were the most important codes to know, I had hoped to get them to be critical about that practice. As our staff discussion continued, I made sure to prompt them with questions about when, how, and for whom certain affects were considered appropriate.

In response to the question about the most common affects, tutors talked about Interest, Affection, and Validation, but they also identified several negative affects such as Stonewalling (particularly for students required to come to sessions) and Fear/Tension (especially during high-stakes periods or assignments). By and large, they intuited Interest and Validation as being important for building rapport with writers and making the session comfortable enough for the writers to experiment with their writing. They also felt these two codes were crucial as responses to writer affects such as Anger and Fear/Tension. These approaches were interesting to me as they indicated the tutors were not only identifying these common features of the genre but also displaying a fuller emotional literacy—making "use of relationships with others to better understand and process emotional information" (Alemdar & Anilan, 2022, p. 30). The codes provided them a language with which to label instances of their partner's affect; they could, in turn, use (monitor, regulate) their affect to regulate their partner's.

The tutors identified a great deal of overlap between what they thought were the most common affect cues and those that were most important. Once again, Interest and Validation were considered crucial given the importance of rapport and trust in the session. Validating student frustration was a prominent topic in the discussion, but several negative cues were identified as equally important, particularly regarding Validation. For instance, some discussed how important it was to identify instances of Fear/Tension and Defensiveness so they would know how to Validate those feelings. Others noted the fine line they would have to walk in giving feedback without accidentally crossing over into Criticism. They also considered how they might balance Validating a writer's concerns without making those feelings the focus of the session. Most of the tutors felt that it was acceptable to show "negative" affects as a form of empathy or mirroring (and thus an indicator of Affection).

At the end of the workshop, I asked them to consider, in future sessions, who in the session is permitted to show "negative" affect, and how race, class, ability, and other intersections of identity inflect that performance. I also invited them to think about how intercultural communication might be facilitated or impeded by the assumptions embedded in the SPAFF. My hope here is that we can continue these conversations in workshops like what I outline below. We have planned on viewing sample sessions now that our staff has a passing familiarity with the terms.

WORKSHOPS

Even prior to fully adapting the SPAFF for writing center uses, I was able to take elements from it for workshops. Over the last few years, I've offered variations of a workshop that asked participants to consider body language, personal space, and affect as genre features. I've conducted this workshop at my own center, at another center, and a few years ago during a regional writing center conference. I begin by sharing a 5-minute YouTube video of a sample writing center session. I use this specific video because it illustrates a lot of problematic issues with white male embodiment in sessions. I hesitate here to share many specifics about the video because I don't want to disparage the center that published it. However, the video description indicates that "the goal of this video series is to present writing center best practices to future tutors." I use this video also because although it is scripted, I am less concerned with getting a truly representative example of practice than I am in how the participants labor to convey what they imagine to be the preferred display affect of their roles in a video seeking "to present writing center best practices." Both actors were also tutors in that writing center. Accordingly, viewers are watching what that center and those tutors believe to be the proper countenance, sponsored by a well-established center. In short, their practice is considered normal and ostensibly valued by the community. I share it here not as a critique or commentary about this center or its values but rather to show how an interrogation of affect and the nonverbal features of the peer tutoring session can reveal attitudes about who is authorized to use the genre of the writing center session.

The video itself shows two men seated roughly side-by-side in what appears to be a writing center. The tutor is an older, taller man and the writer is a college-age younger man. The writer seems a bit nervous and explains that he has composed a first draft for his professor. The tutor peers over his glasses, leveling his head down as he does so, asking the writer what he would like to work on. The writer emphasizes grammar, spelling, and academic voice. They set an agenda wherein the tutor emphasizes that they will focus on organization and the thesis, insisting that that's what the professor will look for in the first draft. He says that if they do that, the writing will "sound natural."

An icon appears on the screen to indicate that time has passed, transitioning to the next instance of interaction in the session. The tutor mentions that they had worked on organization together and then corrects the student on an agreement error, asking the student if it was the study the student was writing about that got cancer rather than the mice, laughing at his own joke afterward. They work through the error, after which the tutor hands the writer the pencil he's been holding so that the writer can make the adjustment, telling him to "write that down." The screen momentarily fades to black, indicating another time transition. They appear to be wrapping up the session, the tutor indicating what the writer should do ahead of the due date, telling him, "Alright. Here's what you're going to work on." The writer once again raises his concerns about voice, which the tutor insists is something they can work on later, insisting that "that's not the most important . . . the writing is understandable. It's clear, okay?" After some further discussion of what the tutor decided the writer's priorities should be the writer asks, "So it is better to have details before the grammar?" and when the tutor affirms this, the writer sighs and leans back, seemingly defeated. The tutor then aggressively shakes the writer's hand, saying "Good luck!" to which the writer sighs and says "thank you" somewhat quietly. The video then ends.

In the two staff meetings I've used this activity in, I tried not to spoil (so to speak) the nature of the exercise so that I could get participants' unbiased thoughts. After watching the video, I asked them for their impressions. Many students among both staffs felt that the tutor was correct to focus on HOCs rather than LOCs and that he seemed to do his best to comfort the nervous writer. However, some women in those meetings felt that the tutor "took up a lot of space" and seemed to dominate the session somehow. In both meetings (and in a later conference talk), after discussing initial impressions, I briefly reviewed concepts such as proxemics, vocal tone, backchanneling (a potential indicator of Validation or Domineering), sentence types (declarative, imperative, and interrogative), and different sorts of questions (content clarification, comprehension checking, and/or politely stated directives). I shared a handout to help draw audience members' attention to these and other—more embodied—features of the session genre. The handout contained the following questions:

- What do the duo's body language, posture, proxemics/personal space, and tone/volume tell you about how each of them configures his role in the session? Why do you think that?

- Who controls the pencil and paper? Why might that matter?
- Please consider the consultant's use of backchanneling. Does he use it to affirm the writer's thoughts, ideas, and/or questions, or is it used to assert the tutor's control of the session? What makes you think that?
- Please consider the types of sentences the consultant uses: declarative, imperative, interrogative. Do you find any types more troubling than other types in the session? How do these types of sentences (and their use) determine who directs the session?
- How is the consultant using questions? For clarifying content and/or rhetorical decisions? For comprehension checking? For politely phrasing directives? Why might this matter?

In each of the sessions, we then watched the video again, pausing at certain points to let participants record their thoughts. After the video concluded, participants then shared what they wrote, many struck by how their perceptions of the dynamics of the session had changed. For instance, many of the women in both groups commented on how the tutor seemed to "manspread," taking up a lot of the physical space in the session, forcing the writer to cede some of the area around his paper. Others remarked on how the tutor intruded into the writer's downcast field of view to force unsolicited eye contact or point his finger into the writer's personal space.

They also noted how the tutor controlled the pencil throughout, using it as a focus to direct the writer's attention in imperatives such as "Take a look here. Find me the verb in this sentence" or "Here's what you're going to work on" and "Remember: you're going to add some more details to your argument." The audience remarked on several more of these imperatives used throughout. And though these imperatives were somewhat startling on their own, audience members remarked on how they were often combined with the tutor's aggressive body language. For instance, at one point, the tutor says, "We need to make sure that the organization is good and that the argument is good and then *later* [nearly touches the writer with a sort of abbreviated chopping motion to emphasize that word] we can focus on grammar."

In these workshops, I followed up on participants' observations to explain some of the SPAFF constructs such as Interest, Domineering, and Defensiveness. For example, as we discussed backchannels, I pointed out that they are typically *indicators* of Validation. That is, they "communicate sincere understanding and acceptance of one's partner or of one's partner's views and opinions" (Coan & Gottman, 2007, p. 280). However, "bobbing heads" and "interrupting" are *counterindicators* of Validation, more in line with negative affective behaviors such as Domineering or Defensiveness. We then talked about how the tutor used backchanneling to interrupt or (in the case of head bobbing) communicate impatience—what Coan and Gottman (2007) described as "a kind of nonverbal request to 'shut up'" (p. 280).

Participants also noted how Domineering indicators showed up in the tutor's body language. For instance, participants in all the sessions pointed out how the tutor lowered his head to not only invade the writer's personal space but also impose eye contact as well. Given the angle of his head, then, the tutor had to look over his glasses, with his chin down. Coan and Gottman (2007) defined this physical indicator as "glowering," which is "really a kind of steady gaze, often characterized by the head tilted forward with the chin down, and the outer portions of the eyebrows raised . . . and the person may be leaning the head, body, or both forward" (p. 276). Once attuned to the work of the tutor's gaze and some of the constructs from the SPAFF, participants noted these behaviors much more readily than they had in the first viewing.

These constructs helped inform the workshop discussions in other ways. For instance, many remarked on the tone and even content of some of the tutor's statements, observing the potential negative emotions they might engender in the writer. Several remarked, for example, on the tutor's dismissiveness about the writer's desire to sound natural. When he says, "That's not the most important—the writing is understandable. It's clear, okay?" Accordingly, I introduced the "minimization" *indicator* of Defensiveness. Coan and Gottman (2007) explained that "defensive speakers will frequently try to minimize a complaint by asserting that the problem they are potentially responsible for was scarcely a problem in the first place" (p. 275). Participants then began to identify the ways in which the tutor seemed to regard the writer's assertions of his own goals as a form of complaint, which he then minimized, opting instead to reassert his own authority. Although we didn't observe physical indicators of such, the tutor's verbal indicators alone were enough, then, to give us some insight into his affect. These negative verbal indicators then helped draw attention to other, similar instances.

And though we could have stopped there, I didn't feel the discussion would have been sufficient. After all, to a degree, the workshop enacted a prescriptive approach to genre, implicitly (and sometimes *explicitly*) asking participants to avoid these sorts of behaviors. Rather, my goal was to get them to consider the ways in which bodies and affect empowered or disempowered rhetors from fully enacting agency in that particular rhetorical situation. What the SPAFF and the other question prompts allowed us to do was to identify discrete bits of bodily and verbal behaviors as features of the peer tutoring genre. In so doing, we could then determine how they functioned in directing power.

For the latter part of the workshops, I thus used some of Coe et al.'s (2002) meta-rhetorical questions to prompt further consideration about the genre. Several crucial questions guided our discussion: "Who can—and who cannot—use this genre? Does it empower some people while silencing others?" as well as "What are the political and ethical implications of the rhetorical situation constructed, persona embodied, audience invoked and context of situation assumed by a particular genre?" (Coe et al., 2002, pp. 6–7). These questions are of particular importance when considering body language and affect in the writing center session because they help to tease out the implicit biases and power dynamics inherent in the writing center session.

For example, during the first viewing of the video, most participants did not think much of the older, white, male tutor's habitus—his use of the embodied affective genre features of the session—until we dug into it with that particular focus in mind. Those invasive uses of proximity, those negative affect indicators somehow seemed *natural* to the largely white audience of my workshops. I suspect that much of this is due to how older, white males are typically viewed in the academy: as bodies always-already encoded with authority, with privilege. Once we began to look specifically at the way he occupied that space with his body, however, participants began to see how their expectations anticipated and were shaped by that authority.

We began to interrogate this idea further, asking participants to imagine different subject positions for the writer and tutor, while keeping their roles the same. Though many of the audience in each workshop seemed uncomfortable addressing race directly, most could not imagine, for instance, a Black man being able to occupy a habitus in the same way as the tutor in this video, affirming Sévère's (2019) discussions of the way Black male bodies are encoded in these spaces. Further, when imagining the writer in this session as a Black man, most took especial umbrage to the tutor's habitus, demonstrating how being in bodies as a genre feature of the session is always-already raced.

Similarly, these spaces are always-already gendered. The majority of the workshop participants presented as women, and they were much more vocal about the ways sex and gender were clearly enacted and embodied in the tutor's habitus. Across all three workshops, women pointed out the tutor's manspreading behaviors and clear entitlement to the space. When discussing his use of backchanneling behaviors to interrupt the writer, several women remarked on having similar experiences.

In sum, the way that tutors and writers are positioned—both in their roles in the session and in the intersectionalities they occupy—can overdetermine their ability to "be" in the genre. Of course, peer tutoring *is* asymmetrical and certain aspects of this asymmetry can and should be used to help writers traverse difficult learning tasks. That said, asymmetry can manifest and be reinforced in ways beyond the overly simple "directive/nondirective" binary that too often structures discourse around power dynamics in the session (Kjesrud, 2015). Rather, we would be remiss to not consider how the inherent power imbalances in the tutor/writer dynamic impact and are impacted by the circulation of affect in and around the session: how embodiment in this genre authorizes certain bodies. Put still another way, how do the embodied features of the peer tutoring genres reinforce the normalization or primacy of a white, male, straight, cisgender habitus? Although these workshops only began those sorts of conversations, the contrast between participants' initial impressions and their impressions after considering affect were markedly different. Accordingly, a more genre-oriented examination of affect in the session could be particularly powerful for those interested in social justice work in the center and in interrogating the roles affect and emotion play in equity in the center.

Conclusion: Better Sponsors of (Embodied) Literacy

Ultimately I hope that tutors fluent in many of the SPAFF codes will be more attuned to the emotions that drive those displays. For instance, a tutor noticing themself feeling angry may realize that, according to the SPAFF, Anger tends to emerge from a perceived violation of one's right to autonomy or respect. They may then be able to consider the perceived violation and its origin. Is it merely an instance of being rude or is it a microaggression? The tutor can then adjust their practice and address the affront more generatively and purposively. The same could be said for instances of Defensiveness or Domineering: a tutor, fluent in the codes, may find themself unintentionally displaying these affects, and that fluency can lead to a moment of consideration, to listening to their body and its own rhetoric. My hope is that rather than simply surface acting or deep acting, tutors fluent in the SPAFF may be able to both feel *and* display their feelings, addressing them generatively and appropriately within the contexts of the session. Imagine, for instance, how powerful a moment it would be if in the sample video we examined the tutor were to catch himself and address the behavior with the student: "You know, I want to apologize. I realize I've been intruding into your space and dismissing some of your concerns. Can I ask how you'd like to proceed, and what I might do to better address those concerns?" Such moments would require both vulnerability and empathy. Imagine if we reconfigured the preferred display affect of tutoring sessions to not only allow for such moments *but to expect them.*

And with any dimension of literacy learning, I think it's important to consider the sponsorship dimension of that literacy and the implications of that sponsorship for ethical practice. The concept of literacy sponsorship comes from Deborah Brandt (2001), who defines *sponsors* as "any agents, local or distant, concrete or abstract, who enable, support, teach, and model, as well as recruit, regulate, suppress, or withhold, literacy—and gain advantage by it in some way" (p. 19). In the case of traditional alphabetic literacy, these sponsors might comprise teachers, family members, supervisors, friends, or others. In the case of the exercise above, I have thus acted as a sponsor of a particular form of literacy. The training manuals, videos, and other materials we use are forms of sponsorship, and any time WCDs train for body language and affect, they too act as sponsors.

As Brandt (2001) characterized it, sponsors "lend their resources or credibility to the sponsored but also stand to gain benefits from their success, whether by direct payment or, indirectly, by credit of association" (p. 19). If the act of navigating, negotiating, and responding to the meanings that emerge from bodies interacting constitutes a form of literacy, a sponsor has something to gain from propagating that literacy. Accordingly, I think sponsorship serves as another useful metaphor for writing center practitioners for considering what we gain in exploring and propagating this literacy, and for considering what we or others might stand to lose.

And to be clear, I don't feel that my concerns here are insurmountable. Indeed, issues of regulatory power and literacy sponsorship have been generatively engaged and addressed in the context of the composition classroom and in the writing center. And though Brandt (2001) stresses that sponsors have something to gain by their sponsorship, as Eli Goldblatt (2007) has explained, it does not have to be an unfair situation:

> As long as the partners come to know each other well enough to recognize where they share interests and where their interests diverge . . . it is possible for them to sponsor literacy jointly for a particular group or groups; all can benefit and none need to feel subordinated or exploited. (p. 140)

I believe the key here is that the stakes surrounding that literacy need to be spelled out—among both sponsors and those sponsored.

Finally, I would like briefly to consider a final implication of what I've outlined here with the idea of self-care. Hochschild (2013) has asked if emotional labor can be fun, discussing care workers and how sometimes they enjoyed their work in spite of (or even because of) the challenges that come with emotional labor. Hochschild (2013) has pointed out that there are several reasons people engage with that labor. Maybe we can prompt tutors to consider what they enjoy about that labor as part of the training. Part of training for emotional labor is training to understand how to enjoy it and identify what's enjoyable about it. And a critical genre pedagogy implores us to consider *who* gets to enjoy it and how we might listen to our bodies to understand those feelings.

Mindfulness is thus both necessary for and a result of practice guided by affect. One of the principles advocated by Beaufort (2007) regarding the acquisition and transfer of rhetorical knowledge is to "teach the practice of mindfulness, or metacognition, to facilitate positive transfer of learning" (p. 182). Mindfulness has been gaining some traction in rhetoric and composition studies in recent years, and it has begun to appear in writing center studies as well, with figures such as Bill McAuley starting a mindfulness discussion group to develop and explore potential research questions and collaborations on the topic. I believe mindfulness may be a way to answer Johnson et al.'s (2015) call to "recontextualize bodies as entities with their own rhetorical agency" in that mindfulness asks us to listen to our bodies not as objects but as their own rhetorical agents. In essence, this approach may offer us a research and practice path that enables us to de-center the logocentric subject in writing center practice and diffuse agency, giving bodies their rhetorical due. At the same time, it can help consultants (and directors and writers) listen to and articulate their understanding of bodies and the so-called nonverbal to better engage in the self-care so necessary for sustainable writing center practice. Workshops such as what Godbee et al. (2015) described are one way to assist writers in becoming more mindful of their bodies. My hope is that genre-oriented approaches such as I've described here might still be another.

In sum, I wish to reaffirm Anis Bawarshi's (2000) call to rhetoric and composition scholars and extend it to writing center practitioners when he asks for us to allow the genre function to

> expand and synthesize our field of inquiry to include the constitution of all discourses and the identities implicated within them, thereby helping us to rethink our at times unhealthy distinctions . . . and focus instead on how

all texts, writers, and readers are constituted by the genres in which they function. (p. 358)

Here I would add to this call those nonverbal texts—or rather, those embodied representations—that compose our writing center praxis and for us to rethink the unhelpful distinctions between body and text that have inhibited our understanding of this genre.

More Than Just Our Centers

This book has been layered with stories: the individual case studies, the anecdotes about staff meetings, the conversations with writers and tutors, and more. And stories need closure, but I'm afraid I have little to offer here. I would love to say that our staff's training in the wake of this research has led to more meaningful affective practice, but I don't know that—yet. We're working in-house on pre- and post-test assessments of affective practice based on our training interventions, and I'm still considering what a more qualitative approach might look like.

It would mean the world to me to say that we can now prepare our new tutors to deal with anxiety during their first session, but we have so much else to prioritize that sometimes this sort of emotion work is deferred. I would like to think that our discussions about emotional labor have alleviated potential stress and burnout among our staff, but this work is an ongoing process. What I do know, however, is that without this intervention and focusing on affect and emotions through the framework of the SPAFF, my staff and I would not have the shorthand necessary to describe the critical but often underexamined work that we do in the writing center.

And, truth be told, such work can't be limited to our centers alone. As Ahmed (2004) has described, affect circulates. Its effects are felt throughout

https://doi.org/10.7330/9781646428649.c005

the various networks to which the writing center is tied. If we wish to limit the toll exacted by emotional labor in our centers, we need to work beyond them to help facilitate more just and sustainable emotional labor within them. Here, then, in this book's conclusion I wish to consider what forms of outreach and advocacy we might do in this regard, what questions remain, and what stances we might adopt in our practice and research. I would also like us to reconsider some of our stories: the stories we tell others to define ourselves and the work that we do in writing centers as well as the stories we tell ourselves.

Emotional labor in the center is always inflected by external pressures, and these stories frame that labor. Moreover, tutors must navigate the contradictions inherent in this work: to be justice-oriented but also to serve the interests of the faculty members (and institutions) to which the writers are subject; to "make better writers" in these contexts even as they are aware that the very construct of "better writers" is raced, classed, and gendered. Reconciling these contradictions can thus lead to still more emotional labor and the sorts of cynicism and burnout I described in Chapter 3.

It seems clear to me, then, that we need different ways of engaging other stakeholders, of helping to set expectations around what writing is and what occurs in the center. But we also need to further study and learn from tutors and administrators who do this work, day in and day out, for better and for worse. Some of the research on burnout would benefit from deeper examination of the affective and emotional labor necessary to do the job, but there also needs to be better training and support for tutors and WCAs and practitioners about the tensions in our work. It is precisely because of the material model under which most writing centers in the US labor—through contingent and highly mobile staffs of undergraduate and graduate tutors—that we need to invest specifically in training to prepare tutors for tensions and conflict in their tutoring work. As a profession, we owe it to our workers, and, as an economic model that underpins the university, our labor demands upskilling that enhances tutor labor and makes it more sustainable and enjoyable. We need new stories, and I believe the SPAFF can provide some of the words.

Messaging, Affect, and Our Institutions

Perhaps our most common narratives in the field are those we tell our institutional partners to help set expectations about what it is that we do. Perhaps we say we are for any writer at any stage of the writing process; that we're not an editing service; that we are inclusive spaces; that we do faculty development;

that we are good stewards of our budget or a great return on investment that helps students to persist and thrive in college. But misapprehension about writing centers among the greater institution is as old as the field itself, and that misapprehension has an impact on emotional labor within the center. Writing center workers have described the emotional drag of being seen as "paper-in, paper-out," of being at the whim of a revolving door of administrators with short attention spans, of being part of a system that prioritizes "stacking them cheap to educate them cheap" (Giaimo & Lawson, 2024, p. 88). The stories that we tell often include emotional and affective valances; more often than that, these stories appear banal and procedural but are informed and underwritten by emotion. The forms of emotional labor we carry out are in no small way shaped by perceptions of the writing center; those perceptions are in turn often affective in nature.

Largely, writing center studies scholars have approached the problem of faculty misperceptions as either a matter of education and/or a matter of rhetoric (Carino, 2001; North, 1984; Pemberton, 1992; Harris, 2010). That is, if confronted with a clearer, more persistent, or more persuasive case for what writing center work is, stakeholders outside the center will adjust their perceptions in kind. I believe, however, that typical rhetorical approaches to representing the writing center are insufficient because they fail to grapple with something more foundational to perceptions of writing center work: that beliefs about writing are fundamentally ideological and constitutive—they are *affective*. And though I agree with Harris (2010) and others that defining ourselves in terms of negatives (e.g., "we are not a fix-it shop") can backfire, so too can defining ourselves in terms of positives (e.g., "we work with all writers with any of their needs")—even if we are doing so on our own terms.

This is because any articulation or definition of writing center work necessarily—implicitly or explicitly—articulates or defines *writing*. In doing so, they necessarily present many faculty with a counter-narrative of sorts to what are often deeply held ideologies about writing (and thus about the larger world). Often seemingly innocuous notions about correctness or about the center, such as what Pemberton (1992) has characterized as the "clinic, madhouse, or prison," are not necessarily discrete misapprehensions. Rather, they can be symptomatic of larger and more constitutive ideologies around language and identity. And as studies have demonstrated (Kahan, 2013; Nyhan & Reifler, 2010), when presented with information conflicting with deeply held beliefs, a subject will go to great lengths to refute that information, to rationalize the beliefs, and/or resolve the cognitive dissonance that the new facts engender without changing to accommodate the new information. In essence, presenting someone with evidence counter to those beliefs can actually *strengthen* them. So long as we define ourselves in terms of what we offer the university, we continue to butt up against these ideologies.

I believe misapprehensions of the writing center persist because the autonomous model of literacy is still the guiding model of the neoliberal university. As Street (2006) has described it,

> The standard view in many fields, from schooling to developmental programmes, works from the assumption that literacy in itself—autonomously—will have effects on other social and cognitive practices. . . . The model, I suggest, disguises the cultural and ideological assumptions that underpin it so that it can be presented as though they are neutral and universal and that literacy as such will have these benign effects. (p. 1)

Literacy and (by extension) writing are thus imagined to be neutral tools independent of the social actors involved in its transmission. I would also argue that such a conception of literacy can be disciplinary in nature. That is, in addition to normalizing white languaging practices as standard, typical pedagogical practices in the university also imagine disciplinary norms to be standard as well.

Consider, for instance, a white male cisgender heterosexual faculty member from the Midwest in a STEM-related field. Because of white supremacist language practices in the United States, this faculty member's home language practices have been reified as normal or somehow merely a transparent vehicle indicative of the person's cognitive clarity. That is, rather than being situated as one dialect among many variations of English, this person's home dialect has been instantiated as the only proper dialect: it is definitionally Standard Written English. This hypothetical faculty member's work is assessed in terms of that very dialect, and in fact that dialect becomes the very means by which to even engage in discussion about the work of dialect more broadly conceived. The common or dominant then becomes the standard.

Accordingly, this person's ability to perform in the academy using this language directly benefits from the perpetuation of the autonomous model of literacy. This model has served this faculty member very well and is likely bound up in that faculty member's sense of identity. This faculty member thus has an especial investment in an individualist ideology that can at once explain his accomplishments at the same time as serve as a sort of alibi to absolve him of any complicity in a system that uses language as a form of colonialism on his students. If English literacy were simply a neutral tool, then it stands to reason that those who haven't been as successful with language practices in the academy are failing as individuals rather than as casualties of hegemonic institutional practices. This is where the writing center often comes into play: in between the assumptions of faculty and standards of the institution that are not only de facto but de novo.

It is only natural then that such a faculty member would turn to the writing center to "fix" "deficient" students. Accordingly, as Grimm (2011) has described, it is exactly this sort of ideology that perpetuates linguistic hegemony and white supremacy. By focusing on fixing individuals, we ignore larger concerns—we "come to facile and judgmental conclusions such as 'some students just don't work hard enough,' or 'some students just aren't motivated enough,'" and so on (p. 78). And lest I seem to be creating a sort of straw person in this hypothetical STEM faculty member, recent research has found that

> while . . . racial achievement gaps are determined by multiple (e.g., economic and structural) factors, they may be exacerbated by subtle situational cues from STEM professors that reinforce racial stereotypes about which social groups are more or less likely to have ability in STEM. (Canning et al., 2019)

If the autonomous model of literacy imagines literacy to be a neutral tool, faculty who subscribe to it are also more likely to enact this fixed mindset. And as Canning et al. (2019) have found,

> fixed mindset professors are more likely to judge a student as having low ability based on a single test performance and to use unhelpful pedagogical practices, like encouraging students to drop difficult courses (e.g., 'not everyone is meant to pursue a STEM career').

Often these situational cues can come from and through writing or "unhelpful pedagogical practices" such as what is implicit when a faculty member tells a student that they "need to go to the writing center."

Affect and Outreach in Local Contexts

If we wish to mitigate some of the emotional labor our tutors face in writing center sessions, it's not enough to promote or define writing centers in our institutions. We need to define writing itself, and we need to define it in terms of race, class, and intersectionality. But more, we need to engage in the affective work necessary to define it to stakeholders who may be quite resistant to that discourse. And if, as I assert, orientations toward writing are ideological, we need more than "sticky" rhetoric to change perceptions of our work. As Alcorn (2002) explained it,

> human subjects, while they do show multiple and conflicting identities, also reveal defensive resistances to discourse manipulation.... Something within a subject operates to preserve and maintain a characteristic identity. This mechanism (much of psychoanalytic theory describes it in terms of libidinal attachments and defensive subject functions) prompts subjects to actively challenge rather than passively internalize the discourse they are given ... they work repetitively and defensively to represent identity. (p. 17)

In the case of writing center outreach to faculty, those faculty may be capable of acknowledging what we try to tell them, but these faculty members may still require students to come to the center to be corrected, vetted, or made to sound less like a user of their home dialect. What faculty experience every day—as writers themselves whose workload is reduced by sending students to the center conflicts with the frame of writing we often hope to impart in and about our centers. Their prior practices and beliefs make negotiating the discursive terrain of their world and working lives easier and more consistent with their beliefs. As a result, they may privilege those practices and beliefs over our arguments for what writing is and its attendant epistemologies.

Alcorn's (2002) solution for addressing the attachments that students have to certain discourses in the composition classroom is bound up in what he refers to as a "pedagogy of mourning"—of grieving: "Because people form libidinal investments in linguistic constructions, optimum flexibility in discourse use requires painful acts of libidinal disinvestment that analysts describe as mourning" (p. 110). In brief, for people to part with discourses that are integral to their sense of identity, they need spaces in which they can imagine new subject positions. They are, in essence, giving up a piece of themselves, and this work is inherently affective. Consequently, this can be difficult work for writing centers, particularly if our only, or primary, frame is that of the standard orientation session or if faculty members' conception of us comes only through our standard promotional materials—that is, through our public-facing rhetoric. I believe outreach must be more personal and located in vulnerability, where faculty can "grieve" for subject positions they formerly occupied and can let go of. This isn't to say we shouldn't advertise our services. Of course we should. We should also engage in the sorts of rhetoric that promote and define our services. After all, not all faculty are beholden to the autonomous model of literacy, and for those who are not, the writing center can provide a lifeline of sorts for those who partner with it. I do believe, however, that there are more efficacious spaces in which we can tackle this ideology. In my own practice, I have found two approaches to be successful in my institutional outreach: through writing across the curriculum work centered around exploring threshold concepts and through partnerships with diversity, equity, and inclusion (DEI) professional development efforts for faculty.

I have worked with faculty from different disciplines in our Writing Center Advisory Council and through WAC workshops on the topic of threshold concepts. In brief, threshold concepts are those ideas that, as Adler-Kassner and Wardle (2015) have explained, "learners must 'see through and see with' (Kreber, 2009, p. 11) in order to participate more fully in particular disciplines" (ix). The defining characteristics of threshold concepts as characterized by Meyer and Land (2006) are that they are troublesome, liminal, integrative and transformative, and probably irreversible. Threshold concepts invite us to consider how disciplinary knowledge is rooted in subjectivity—not that such knowledge is relative, but in how that knowledge shapes subjectivity and in how subjectivity inflects learners' encounters with that knowledge. Positing writing studies as a discipline with its own threshold concepts can thus provide faculty a space in which to grapple with their own subjectivity and ways of making meaning through writing.

Cross-discipline faculty professional development around threshold concepts is invaluable in that as faculty identify and articulate the threshold concepts of their particular disciplines, they encounter others doing the same. Because they are navigating the concepts in their own discipline that outsiders may find alien, troubling, and/or transformative, they begin to create subject positions for themselves as they encounter these same concepts in regard to writing studies and other disciplines. Moreover, they can more readily empathize with student (and hopefully writing center) encounters with language practices as they themselves encounter difference along several epistemological and ontological axes. There have been powerful moments when discussing these concepts and how students encounter them that I have been able to break through and speak to dialect, class, and race and how these further inflect those learning encounters. Wardle (2019) described her own efforts in faculty development:

> Faculty also try to name characteristics of "good" writing in their own disciplines, and teach these to colleagues from other disciplines. They quickly come to recognize that what makes writing "good" varies quite a lot by

context. These disciplinary differences underscore that teaching students to write across the university takes sustained effort and time, and is everyone's shared responsibility. (IHE)

I have found that these conversations shift our focus away from the idea of writing as a universal skill to writing as a situated practice. Accordingly, as Greenfield (2019) has found, "if faculty are focused on the idea of writing as merely a technical process or skill, it is difficult to argue about the role of a peer mentor as anything other than someone who provides a remedial service" (p. 94). In this regard, threshold concepts have been invaluable in my work prompting a more reflective stance on writing and faculty members' own experience with it. In turn, such a stance has helped me to clarify the center's positionality and some of the frictions tutors encounter in navigating faculty expectations.

Similarly, I've been able to work alongside our Office of Diversity Education to conduct workshops with faculty on how seemingly innocuous activities like correcting and responding to student writing can have significant ramifications in mediating student identity. I've been especially glad to be a part of these panels because the panels weren't directly (or solely) about writing pedagogy. As a result, I've been able to interact with faculty members I otherwise wouldn't have in my role as the writing center's director. And more, I could talk to them about writing without it being a direct result of their practices (which can often read as an indictment of those practices). I've also served on panels on topics such as inclusive language in the classroom and on bias in communication.

One thing I've done at each is to begin my part by reciting the CCC's "Statement on Students' Right to Their Own Language." I then ask participants when they would guess the statement was drafted. Most participants guess within the last decade or so. When I tell them the actual date—1974—most are surprised. I then explain that our field has strived to move past notions of "correct" language for longer than I have been alive, but that often so much of teaching writing in the university is unfortunately about Standard Written English. I then share bits about assimilationist versus accommodationist approaches to teaching English and my own development as a composition teacher. In modeling this sort of vulnerability, I invite participants to reciprocate.

In these panels, we have been able to have conversations about language norms and unwitting assimilationist and colonial practices in responding to student writing. Faculty often remarked at their own feelings of guilt or worry about culpability in inadvertently contributing to an intellectual culture of repression. We also have discussed the tension between teaching students to write in an environment where other professors will hold students to a White English standard and what they might do to help students preserve their linguistic and cultural identities. One thing I've done in these workshops to capitalize on these kairotic moments is to discuss the role the writing center can (and does) play in enabling students to acknowledge and call out Standard Written English as one dialect among many and to acknowledge the validity of their home dialects and language practices. In turn, this has invited faculty to reconsider the center as an intellectual and affective space for this work rather than merely as an extension of their own linguistic authority.

These spaces have been far more generative for transformative conversations about writing than the most well-designed pamphlet or carefully worded email. Our promotion efforts are important, but these vulnerable, one-on-one encounters with faculty members on writing, disciplinarity, and positionality can have profound impacts on the sorts of emotional labor needed in our centers. The SPAFF can also provide WPAs and WCDs like me a way to read the room in these contexts, to identify the sorts of affect circulating and address it appropriately. I have learned, for instance, in my own experience to recognize Defensiveness—both in myself and others—in these conversations. I can then consider its cause and how (and whether) to broach it. In short, the SPAFF has provided me with tools to more adequately perform my own emotional labor.

Emotional Labor and Advocacy in Broader Contexts

Genie Giaimo and I (2024) have argued that emotional labor is a form of what we term *metalabor*, which itself is a form of what Arlene Kaplan Daniels (1987) has described as *invisible work*. Daniels (1987) argued that work is often perceived as legitimate—as visible—only if it is public, compensated, and valued. Daniels (1987) focused especially on the invisibility of so-called woman's work, the work of maintaining the conditions necessary for institutions (families, workplaces, organizations) to function. It is typically seen as simply a gendered quality rather than a necessary function, and thus it is not seen or renumerated as valued. Daniels (1987) characterized the "folk understanding" of such work when she explained, "We appreciate and want the efforts that make our institutions more workable though we wouldn't credit most of it as work" (p. 412). In short, invisible work is necessary and allows the ostensible work to occur, but it itself isn't seen, and thus it is not valued.

Giaimo and I (2024) have argued that metalabor is "the work done in order to make working possible, feasible, and/or sustainable" (p. 32). It involves promoting the center, writing reports for administrators, bartering for budget dollars and tutor wages, organizing social groups for employees, and, yes, navigating emotional labor. Metalabor is work for work's sake. All metalabor is invisible work, but not all invisible work is metalabor. Metalabor is done so that the work can occur, and thus emotional labor is a form of metalabor. If we pay tutors to intervene in a writer's process, whether to make "better writers, not better writing," or to assist writers in transfer, or to address linguistic hegemony, or any number of our other ostensible purposes, it is all underwritten by emotional labor. And yet emotional labor is rarely represented in our job descriptions. It's rarely if ever directly addressed in our instructional materials (Lape, 2008; Lawson, 2015; Mannon, 2021) and, as Mannon (2021) has argued, "if we overemphasize helping, caring, and empathizing behaviors when we recruit new tutors, that job description might invoke gender norms and (erroneously and inadvertently) convey that female students are better suited for peer tutoring than male students" (p. 163). This feminization of tutoring work (alongside narratives about the writing center as a home-like space) thus can devalue that work: it seems natural (at least for women) and it is thus invisible.

Instruments like the SPAFF can thus render this invisible work visible. We can see what that work actually looks like. We can train for it *and* advertise for it in our recruitment materials. We can include in our position descriptions things like validating writers, demonstrating interest, being able to identify different affects and respond appropriately for the situation. And we can compensate it. By making this invisible work visible and defining it as *work*, we assign value to it: we legitimize emotional labor. However, as Giaimo and I (2024) have argued, making our labors more visible and legitimizing them requires still more metalabor on the part of administrators and researchers. Admittedly, it can feel like a feedback loop or reinforcing cycle. But it is necessary.

As a field, we might start working to draft sample position descriptions incorporating language borrowed from the SPAFF for directors and others to use in their institutions. We might start conversations about how to better advocate for equitable and sustainable emotional labor conditions throughout our field. The SPAFF can serve as a common tongue of sorts for these conversations, a way for us to keep from talking past one another and to come to some consensus as a field about how this work is valued and why other university stakeholders should care. Once we start normalizing (rather than pathologizing) affective discourses and discourses about affect—that is, once we begin to clearly name how (and what) we feel in the writing center—we may be able to better advocate for that work.

My hope is that work like what I have done in this book extends the conversations we've been having as a field about affect and emotion in the writing center. When I first reviewed the state of the literature in 2015, it was lacking. Since then, we have had an emotional turn. Still, I would like us to capitalize on those conversations and bring attention to the *labor* part of *emotional labor*. More research and far more advocacy is needed—both as a field and as a profession. Giaimo and I (2024) discuss pleasure activism and reconnecting with the joy and passion that brought us to the profession in the first place. And to be clear, emotional labor does not have to be onerous. In fact, it can be fun (Hochschild, 2013; Humphrey et al., 2015). But Hochschild (2013) observed a paradox faced by emotional laborers, particular those in the care professions. In an increasingly neoliberal and bureaucratized world, those laborers may find that in trying to protect their charges (clients, patients, writers) from the harms of this system, they perpetuate that system. The more broken the system, the easier it is to become detached from their labor. The more detached they are, the higher the turnover. The higher the turnover, the more broken the system. For Hochschild (2013), "the alternative to accepting this is to *fix the broken system*. That starts with recognizing the extraordinary emotional labor it takes to maintain a thriving childcare center, nursing home, hospital, or family" (p. 31). Or a writing center. And like Hochschild (2013), I believe such recognition requires a larger movement to improve those conditions and better stories to inform those movements. Tools like the SPAFF may help us facilitate just such.

Modified SPAFF Codes

The following descriptions of each code follow the same format and in many cases very similar verbiage as the original SPAFF. Each code begins with "Functions," describing what the Affect *does* emotionally. "Indicators" provide observable bits of behavior—typically verbal—that can help identify the underlying affect. "Physical Cues" describe facial expressions and body language typically associated with the Affect. These have been significantly simplified from the original SPAFF, foregoing the Action Units identifying discrete physical cues in favor of simply describing physical behaviors associated with that Affect. Finally, "Counterindicators" explain cues that might be mistaken for a given affect and work to clarify how they likely do not originate from that particular Affect.

Affection

FUNCTIONS

Affection shows concern for others and facilitates rapport and bonding. In the original SPAFF, Affection is more specific to exchanges between romantic partners, but we found enough of the core construct relevant to writing center work to keep most of it relatively intact.

https://doi.org/10.7330/9781646428649.c006

INDICATORS

1. **CARING STATEMENTS.** These offer direct statements of care such as "I want to make sure we're using your time well" or "I hope your midterm goes well!"

2. **COMMON CAUSE STATEMENTS.** These cues occur when two or more individuals share affective behavior as a form of trust or bonding. These cues may be followed by affirmations to show solidarity, such as "For sure!" or "Oh, I know!" Comments such as remarking that "I cannot wait for the weekend!" can be coded Affection if intended to express obvious agreement. Even shared "negative" affects can be indicative of common cause if directed at a shared object.

3. **COMPLIMENTS.** Statements that communicate pride in the session partner (e.g., "I really like your attention grabber!" or "This was really helpful.").

4. **EMPATHY.** This occurs when someone reflects their session partner's affect to match (but not mock). Examples may include things such as adapting the gestures or body language of the session partner or echoing the partner's verbiage. Shared smiles are common here.

PHYSICAL CUES

Affection can be indicated by cheek raising and lip corner pull, typically a slight smile.

COUNTERINDICATORS

Sarcasm. Indicators of sarcastic or passive aggression may complicate coding for this category. These usually don't have similar Physical Cues.

Anger

FUNCTIONS

Anger responds to a perceived infringement of a speaker's boundaries. This typically revolves around respect or autonomy, and Anger is often coded as a state of anger without the presence of other "negative" codes such as Belligerence/Contempt or Defensiveness.

INDICATORS

1. **FRUSTRATION.** This can present as a lower-level Anger without verbal components.

2. **ANGRY I-STATEMENTS.** These are direct statements expressing Anger. "I am so angry!" or "I am so frustrated right now!"

3. **ANGRY QUESTIONS OR COMMANDS.** These may seem like verbal indications of other codes (or Neutral), but the underlying affect indicates irritation or indignation. "Why?!" or "Why won't you edit this for me?!" "Why won't you just incorporate the suggestion?!" or "I don't need help with that!"

PHYSICAL CUES

The lips often narrow, pressing tightly together. Teeth may clench, while muscles in the jaw and neck may become tense. The voice might abruptly rise in pitch, volume, and speed, sometimes accompanied by a "growl" akin to yelling.

COUNTERINDICATORS

Anger can sometimes mix with other codes; those instances should be coded as the other Affect.

Belligerence/Contempt

FUNCTIONS

This code collapses the Belligerence and Contempt codes in the original SPAFF. Belligerence and Contempt are confrontational. They either attempt to provoke Anger or emotionally harm, diminish, or humiliate others. While this could be directed at a tutor or writer, indicators can also be reserved for those outside the session: instructors, family, roommates, and so on.

INDICATORS

1. **TAUNTING QUESTIONS.** These often display as repetitive, irritating questions like "Why can't you?" or "Why don't you make me?"

2. **UNRECIPROCATED AND/OR HOSTILE HUMOR.** Sarcastic or self-oriented jokes that are unreciprocated by the listener are never coded as Humor. They may, however, be coded as Belligerence/Contempt.

3. **INTERPERSONAL TERRORISM.** This is a form of boundary transgression (thus provoking Anger in the listener). This might look like statements such as "What would you do if I did?" or "What are you going to do about it?" "Don't interrupt me!" as a means of demonstrating power.

4. **CONTEMPTUOUS BEHAVIOR.** This can consist of sarcasm, mockery, insults, and similar behavior.

PHYSICAL CUES

Eye-rolling is typically coded as contempt and belligerence. Eyebrows may be raised, and the lips may be pulled to the side.

COUNTERINDICATORS

Good natured teasing and jabs shouldn't be counted as this code, particularly if it is shared with the listener.

Criticism

FUNCTIONS

Criticism attacks someone's character (or writing) in a way that is not obviously insulting, as in Belligerence/Contempt. It can often manifest in evaluations of the writer rather than the writing, or as a response to tutor suggestions or methods.

INDICATORS

1. **BLAMING.** This occurs when someone assigns fault, such as "I received a D on that assignment because you didn't edit for me" or "You always add commas where you don't need them" (as opposed to "There are several commas in this sentence that probably aren't necessary").

2. **CHARACTER ATTACKS.** These often manifest as always/never generalizations such as "You guys never give me the feedback I really need."

3. **KITCHEN SINKING.** This typically involves providing a long list of grievances that individually may not "count" as discrete instances of Criticism, but in total function as such. "Every time I come to the writing center, I don't get the help I want, and no one listens to me. I failed my last paper . . ."

4. **NEGATIVE MIND READING.** Statements such as these make negative assumptions about the listener's intent, thinking, or actions. "You just think I'm stupid," or "You just don't get it because you're not in Business."

PHYSICAL CUES

N/A.

COUNTERINDICATORS

Insults can sometimes be mistaken for Criticism, though insults that seem to focus on harm would be coded as Contempt/Belligerence.

Defensiveness

FUNCTIONS

Defensiveness looks to avoid blame or accountability and often communicates a certain victimhood. It is often a face-saving mechanism.

INDICATORS

1. **THE "YES, BUT."** These are momentary agreements that shift to disagreements. "Yes, the thesis doesn't forecast that part of the argument, but I don't think it needs to" or "Yes, your paper does address the topic, but it doesn't really have a thesis."

2. **CHANGING THE SUBJECT.** This indicator does not appear in the original SPAFF, but our team of coders often found that Defensive writers or tutors may change the subject to avoid discussing a potentially face-threatening act.

3. **MINIMIZATION.** This occurs when the speaker minimizes an issue they've caused by making it seem like it's not really a problem. "Yes, the essay could be longer, but since it bleeds onto the third page, that technically makes it three pages, so it's fine" or "I don't care; I only need a C" or "Your teacher won't care about that."

4. **EXCUSES.** These indicators find fault, blame, or origin for the speaker's actions elsewhere. "Well, the directions weren't clear, so there was nothing I could do."

5. **AGGRESSIVE DEFENSES.** This can often occur around assessments of potential plagiarism or similarly urgent or egregious ethical issues. "There's still time!" "No, I didn't!"

PHYSICAL CUES

Arms folded across the chest and an increase in pitch and emphasis can indicate Defensiveness.

COUNTERINDICATORS

Sometimes invalidating statements associated with Domineering can be mistaken for Defensiveness.

Disgust

FUNCTIONS

Disgust is an involuntary reaction to an unpleasant trigger.

INDICATORS

1. **INVOLUNTARY REVULSION.** This indicator happens in response to some aversive object, image, or condition. In writing center contexts, involuntary revulsion can sometimes be encountered in writing about medical conditions, lab reports, or other descriptive writing.

2. **MORAL OBJECTION.** In this case, the speaker finds a moral, political, or similar statement or position to be repulsive. This can be encountered in many forms of personal and/or argumentative writing or in response to such.

PHYSICAL CUES

Indicators of Disgust tend to be fairly obvious: the nose may be scrunched as the lips are pulled up and the brow brought down; the speaker may turn their head as if away from the object of Disgust.

COUNTERINDICATORS

Sometimes Disgust maybe be conflated with Anger, Belligerence/Contempt, or Domineering. If the function of a display of Disgust seems to be to disrespect the receiver through insults or similar behavior, it should be coded as Belligerence/Contempt. If an underlying affect of Anger is present, it should be coded as Anger.

Domineering/Threats

FUNCTIONS

The SPAFF describes Threats as "a particularly hostile form of domineering behavior" (280), and they are relatively infrequent in writing center contexts, so I have collapsed it with Domineering here. These behaviors work to control a partner and/or conversation. Domineering behaviors can be accidentally drawn on by tutors trying to direct sessions and manage their dyad partner.

INDICATORS

1. **INVALIDATION.** This behavior contradicts the listener's point of view. "Oh, you are fine! Quit exaggerating" or "Your professor won't care about that."

2. **LECTURING AND PATRONIZING.** Similar to forms of Contempt, this indicator can belittle the listener by disempowering them or their arguments. Appeals to authority, platitudes, and finger pointing can all be indicators of this sort of behavior. "Actually, according to the professor . . ."

3. **LOWBALLING.** These are questions with preconceived answers that work to steer the partner toward a particular action. "You want me to get a good grade, don't you?" or "Don't you want to pass the class?"

4. **INCESSANT SPEECH.** This sort of speech forcibly maintains the conversational floor. The speaker may ignore verbal and nonverbal cues from the partner to speak. It may include finger pointing, interrupting, negative sentence-finishing, and so on.

5. **THREATS AND IF/THEN STATEMENTS.** These statements involve invoking a consequence if the desired action or result doesn't occur. "If I don't get a decent grade, I'm telling my professor you didn't help." "If you don't revise this, you're going to fail."

PHYSICAL CUES

Domineering is often marked by glowering: a steady gaze, head tilted down, eyes at looking up (at the subject) and the outer eyebrows raised in what the SPAFF typically refers to as "the horns." Finger pointing, leaning into another's space, and "manspreading" are often physical manifestations of Domineering behavior.

COUNTERINDICATORS

Good natured teasing or jabs can sometimes look like threats but are more in line with Humor, particularly if reciprocated. Similarly, some forms of patronizing may look like Domineering, but when they serve to insult the listener, they are more properly coded as Belligerence/Contempt.

Enthusiasm

FUNCTIONS

Enthusiasm is a fervent display of interest and/or joy. According to the SPAFF, "Enthusiasm is infectious and often sudden, loud, boisterous, and energetic. Nonverbal behaviors prominently accompany verbal expressions of eagerness and joy" (Coan & Gottman, 2007, p. 276).

INDICATORS

1. **ANTICIPATION.** Anticipation eagerly looks ahead. "Let's go!" "Let's get started!" or "I look forward to it!"

2. **INSPIRATION.** Inspiration can be observed in utterances indicating the writer has been motivated to do, create, or see something in a new way. "I have a great idea now! Let me jot this down!" (with excitement).

3. **POSITIVE SURPRISE, EXCITEMENT, AND/OR JOY.** These are happy reactions indicating pleasure, typically in response to compliments or successfully completing a task, such as "It worked!" or "Oh, thank you so much!"

PHYSICAL CUES

Anticipation might be accompanied by fidgeting and distraction. An upright posture with a general positive affect, along with an increase in pitch and volume, is common. Someone enthusiastic may smile and squint or raise their eyebrows with positive surprise.

COUNTERINDICATORS

Enthusiasm cues can sometimes be mistaken for Interest cues. Coan and Gottman note that "interested questions are accompanied by positive affect of a lower intensity than those coded Enthusiasm" (2007, p. 276). Surprise alone is not a sign of Enthusiasm.

Fear/Tension

FUNCTIONS

Fear and Tension often involuntarily communicate fear, worry, and/or anxiety.

INDICATORS

1. **SPEECH DISTURBANCES.** "Fearful or tense speakers will often have a difficult time expressing or even knowing what they want to say" (Coan & Gottman, 2007, p. 276). Rapid uhs and ahs, as well as possible stuttering are common here. Muttering is also common.

2. **VOCAL PITCH.** The sound or tone of the speaker may get higher. This will typically accompany other indicators.

3. **FIDGETING AND NERVOUS GESTURES.** People experiencing fear or tension will often shift uncomfortably in their seats. They may tug on their

clothes, hair, or hands, or they may bite their lips or the inside of their cheeks. The hands may also seem restless. Sucking air through the teeth is a typical nervous gesture in writing center sessions.

4. **NERVOUS LAUGHTER**. This is typically unshared, and it is often a response to tension.

PHYSICAL CUES

As in item 3 above. Also look for rapidly shifting eye movement, gulping, and a smile without squinting.

COUNTERINDICATORS

Fear and Tension can sometimes be confused for Stonewalling when away behaviors are conflated with fidgeting. Shared nervous laughter can be coded as humor, and some fidgeting behaviors can simply be a Neutral affect for a particular person. Context can inform the coding here.

Humor

FUNCTIONS

The SPAFF defines Humor as sharing "in mutual amusement and joy following a mutually recognized moment of absurdity or fun" (Coan & Gottman, 2007, p. 277). It is important to note that to be coded as Humor, an affective exchange must be mutual: both participants must share the joke, so to speak.

1. **FUN, EXAGGERATION, WIT, AND SILLINESS**. These can be clever observations, jokes, playful behavior, and similar sorts of Humor.

2. **GOOD-NATURED TEASING**. Self-deprecation is common here. It can often be seen in response to a gaffe (in the session or in writing). This is coded as humor *only* when it is shared or when *both* agree about the funniness of the peccadillo.

3. **SUDDEN GIGGLING**. The dyad may begin giggling. Positive valences will accompany this indicator (as opposed to Fear/Tension).

PHYSICAL CUES

Smiling accompanied with squinting and wrinkled foreheads are common in Humor.

COUNTERINDICATORS

Unshared humor should not be coded as Humor. Humor can sometimes be conflated with Fear/Tension (nervous giggling), Affection (when a joke conveys such), or Belligerence/Contempt (when used to bully).

Interest

FUNCTIONS

Interest communicates genuine interest in the session partner through active elaboration or clarification-seeking beyond mere information exchange.

INDICATORS

1. **NONVERBAL ATTENTION WITH POSITIVE AFFECT.** Nonverbal behaviors such as leaning forward in their chair, warm tone of voice, steady eye contact with the *session partner or text*. Note the SPAFF focuses on steady eye contact with a partner; however, writing center sessions are less intimate and participants are usually seated side by side to look at a text.

2. **ELABORATION AND CLARIFICATION-SEEKING.** Paraphrasing *questions* (Interest) are easy to confuse with paraphrasing *statements* that are coded as Validation (discussed later). Questions associated with Interest might include "Was that frustrating for you?" or "Am I making sense?" or "So are you saying that logistics were the primary factor for the North's success?"

3. **OPEN-ENDED QUESTIONS.** Per the SPAFF, "Almost any question that does not require a 'yes' or 'no' response and that allows the partner to express [themself] in greater detail" is an indicator of Interest (Coan & Gottman, 2007, p. 278).

PHYSICAL CUES

Raised eyebrows and a wrinkled forehead are common with Interest along with positive valence markers such as smiling combined with squinting.

COUNTERINDICATORS

There are several counterindicators of Interest that may be more appropriately coded as other affects. Prolonged eye contact, particularly in the context of confrontation or disagreement, may be a form of Belligerence/Contempt or even Stonewalling. Rapid questions leaving the partner no chance to respond may be more properly coded as Belligerence/Contempt or Domineering. Low-balling questions are an example of Domineering, and basic exchanges of facts are Neutral.

Sadness

FUNCTIONS

According to Coan and Gottman, "the Sadness code refers to behaviors that communicate loss, resignation, helplessness, pessimism, hopelessness, or a plaintive or poignant quiescence" (2007, p. 278).

INDICATORS

1. **SIGHING.** Deep sighs are almost always indicators of Sadness, though a sigh of relief is a counterindicator.
2. **POUTING/SULKING.** These are most likely to be seen in the context of someone not getting their way. They can often result in the person withdrawing from the conversation.
3. **RESIGNATION.** This can be communicated through "low energy, slouching, long pauses between words, and so forth" (Coan & Gottman, 2007, p. 279).
4. **CRYING.**

PHYSICAL CUES

Beyond what is enumerated above, the voice may break or tremble. The sad person may hang their heads and/or avert their gaze. A wrinkled forehead accompanied by a frown may indicate Sadness.

COUNTERINDICATORS

Stonewalling can be confused for the pouting indicator of sadness if the person is not responding to their partner via backchanneling. Sighs of relief may accompany the end of Fear/Tension rather than Sadness. Tears of joy, laughter, or affection should not be coded as Sadness.

Stonewalling

FUNCTIONS

Stonewalling communicates "an unwillingness to listen or respond to the receiver" (Coan & Gottman, 2007, p. 279).

INDICATORS

1. **ACTIVE AWAY BEHAVIOR.** These can include cleaning fingernails, looking at split ends, or playing with common personal devices such as cell phones.

2. **NO BACKCHANNELS.** See Validation for backchannels. This behavior can be sudden and very noticeable.

3. **MONITORING GAZE.** This typically means sneaking looks at their partner, as if to prompt them to pay attention to their inattentiveness.

PHYSICAL CUES

As Coan and Gottman explain, "the face will typically appear stiff or frozen. The jaw may be clenched, and the muscles of the neck may be obviously flexed" (Coan & Gottman, 2007, p. 279). Otherwise, they may show no obvious physical cues at all.

COUNTERINDICATORS

Stonewalling can sometimes be confused for other affects or states such as boredom, sleepiness, or resignation (which may be coded as Sadness).

Validation

FUNCTIONS

As Coan and Gottman explain, "the function of Validation is to communicate sincere understanding and acceptance of one's partner or of one's partner's views and opinions" (2007, p. 280).

INDICATORS

1. **BACKCHANNELS.** These consist of active listening behaviors such as head nods, uh-huhs, and showing thumbs up.

2. **DIRECT EXPRESSIONS OF UNDERSTANDING.** Utterances confirming the listener understands: "I agree" or "That's a very good point."

3. **PARAPHRASING.** This behavior consists of repeating what the partner says in their own words, such as "So if I understand correctly, you're saying…"

4. **APOLOGIES, GRATITUDE, AND THEIR ACCEPTANCE.** While the original SPAFF focuses on apologies, we find the small rules of interpersonal exchange (thank you, you're welcome, I'm sorry, etc.) to be crucial in validating the session partner.

5. **SENTENCE FINISHING, POSITIVE.** As opposed to cutting their partner off, a person using this indicator will often share and affirm what the speaker says. It is typically accompanied by other indicators of Validation and positive affective cues.

PHYSICAL CUES

In addition to those cues associated with backchanneling, wrinkled foreheads with raised eyebrows or smiling with squinting often accompany Validation.

COUNTERINDICATORS

Counterindicators for Validation can consist of sarcastic backchanneling or bobbing heads (Contempt), empathic mirroring (Affection), or interrupting to seize back the conversational floor (Domineering or Defensiveness).

Whining

FUNCTIONS

Whining is a particular form of complaint. "Whining suggests an innocent victim stance, communicating something like 'What are you picking on me for?'" (Coan & Gottman, 2007, p. 280).

INDICATORS

"Whining is really characterized by a quality of voice paired with a complaint or protest. This voice quality is high-pitched, nasal, 'sing-songy,' or otherwise plaintive. For example, the question 'why' might be expressed in a high-pitched voice and drawn out with an exaggerated 'eeee' sound at the end, as in 'whyyyy-eeee?'" (Coan & Gottman, 2007, p. 280).

PHYSICAL CUES

Sometimes displays of Whining are accompanied by wrinkled foreheads (occasionally with raised eyebrows) and sometimes a frown.

COUNTERINDICATORS

Indicators of Defensiveness can sometimes be uttered in a pitch associated with Whining. The SPAFF recommends coding such as Defensiveness.

Modified SPAFF Handout

Affection shows concern for others and facilitates rapport and bonding.

1. **CARING STATEMENTS.** "I want to make sure we're using your time well," "I hope your midterm goes well!"

2. **COMMON CAUSE STATEMENTS.** "For sure!" or "Oh, I know!" or "Same!"

3. **COMPLIMENTS.** "I really like your attention grabber!" or "This was really helpful."

4. **EMPATHY.** Examples may include things such as adapting the gestures or body language of the session partner or echoing the partner's verbiage.

Anger responds to perceived violations of the speaker's rights to autonomy and respect. It serves as a kind of "affective underlining" of displeasure and complaint, indicating that an interpersonal boundary has been transgressed.

1. **FRUSTRATION.**

2. **ANGRY I-STATEMENTS.** "I am so angry!" or "I am so frustrated right now!"

3. **ANGRY QUESTIONS OR COMMANDS.** "Why?!" or "Why won't you edit this for me?!" "Stop!" or "I don't need help with that!"

continued on next page

https://doi.org/10.7330/9781646428649.c007

Belligerence/Contempt either attempt to provoke Anger or emotionally harm, diminish, or humiliate others. While this could be directed at a tutor or writer, indicators can also be reserved for those outside the session: instructors, family, roommates, etc.

1. **TAUNTING QUESTIONS.** "Why?" (frequent and irritating).

2. **UNRECIPROCATED AND/OR HOSTILE HUMOR.**

3. **INTERPERSONAL TERRORISM.** "What would you do if I did?" or "What are you going to do about it?" "Don't interrupt me!" as a means of demonstrating power.

4. **CONTEMPTUOUS BEHAVIOR.** Sarcasm, mockery, insults, etc.

Criticism attacks someone's character (or writing) in a way that is not obviously insulting, as in Belligerence/Contempt.

1. **BLAMING.** "I received a D on that assignment because you didn't edit for me" or "You always add commas where you don't need them."

2. **CHARACTER ATTACKS.** "You guys never give me the feedback I really need."

3. **KITCHEN SINKING.** "Every time I come to the writing center, I don't get the help I want, and no one listens to me. I failed my last paper."

4. **NEGATIVE MIND READING.** "You just think I'm stupid," or "You just don't get it because you're not in Business."

Defensiveness functions to deflect responsibility or blame. It is often a face-saving mechanism.

1. **THE "YES, BUT."**

2. **CHANGING THE SUBJECT.**

3. **MINIMIZATION.** "Yes, the essay could be longer, but since it bleeds onto the third page, that technically makes it three pages, so it's fine" or "I don't care; I only need a C."

4. **EXCUSES.** "Well, the directions weren't clear, so there was nothing I could do."

5. **AGGRESSIVE DEFENSES.** "I did not!" This can often occur around assessments of potential plagiarism

Disgust is a relatively involuntary verbal or nonverbal reaction to a stimulus that is perceived to be noxious.

1. **INVOLUNTARY REVULSION.** This can sometimes be encountered in writing about medical conditions, lab reports, or other descriptive writing.

2. **MORAL OBJECTION.** Here the object of disgust is an action or idea that the speaker finds repulsive for moral or other symbolic reasons, as in responses to undesirable sexual practices or even political positions.

continued on next page

Domineering/Threats exert and demonstrate control over a partner or conversation.

1. **INVALIDATION.** "Oh, you are fine! Quit exaggerating" or "Your professor won't care about that."

2. **LECTURING AND PATRONIZING.** "Actually, your professor says . . ."

3. **LOW BALLING.** "You want me to get a good grade, don't you?" or "Do you want to pass the class?"

4. **INCESSANT SPEECH.** *It is a form of forcibly maintaining the conversational floor at all times.* Finger pointing, interrupting, negative sentence-finishing, etc.

5. **THREATS AND IF/THEN STATEMENTS.** "If I don't get a decent grade, I'm telling my professor you didn't help."

6. **GLOWERING.**

Fear/Tension often involuntarily communicate fear, worry, anxiety, nervous anticipation, or dread. Often accompanies corrective feedback/critique.

1. **SPEECH DISTURBANCES.** Rapid uhs and ahs, possibly stuttering.

2. **VOCAL PITCH.**

3. **FIDGETING AND NERVOUS GESTURES.**

4. **NERVOUS LAUGHTER.**

Interest communicates genuine interest in the session partner through active elaboration or clarification-seeking beyond mere information exchange.

1. **NONVERBAL ATTENTION WITH POSITIVE AFFECT.** Nonverbal behaviors leaning forward in their chairs, warm tone of voice, steady eye contact with *session partner or text.*

2. **ELABORATION AND CLARIFICATION-SEEKING.** Paraphrasing *questions* (Interest) are easy to confuse with paraphrasing *statements* that are coded as Validation (discussed later). "Was that frustrating for you?" "Am I understanding this correctly?"

3. **OPEN-ENDED QUESTIONS.**

Enthusiasm expresses a passionate interest as well as a positive feeling or outlook associated with that interest.

1. **ANTICIPATION.** "Let's go!" "Let's get started!" or "I look forward to it!"

2. **INSPIRATION.** "I have a great idea now! Let me jot this down!" (with excitement).

3. **POSITIVE SURPRISE, EXCITEMENT, AND/OR JOY.**

Humor shares in mutual amusement and joy following a mutually recognized moment of absurdity or fun. It requires a moment of shared amusement.

1. **FUN, EXAGGERATION, WIT, SILLINESS.**

2. **GOOD-NATURED TEASING.** Self-deprecation is common here.

3. **SUDDEN GIGGLING.**

Sadness refers to behaviors that communicate loss, resignation, helplessness, pessimism, hopelessness, or a plaintive or poignant quiescence.

1. **SIGHING.** Context can often determine whether to code sighing as Sadness or if it is simply neutral.

2. **POUTING/SULKING.** This can be expressed as a generalized reticence or annoyance. Pouting is often associated with thrust-out lips.

3. **RESIGNATION.**

4. **CRYING.**

Stonewalling communicates an unwillingness to listen or respond to the receiver.

1. **ACTIVE AWAY BEHAVIOR.** Cleaning fingernails, looking at split ends or playing with common personal devices such as cell phones.

2. **NO BACKCHANNELS.** (See Validation for backchannels.)

3. **MONITORING GAZE.** Stealing glances at their partners, as if to remind their partners to notice their lack of listening behavior.

Validation communicates sincere understanding and acceptance of one's partner or of one's partner's views and opinions.

1. **BACKCHANNELS.** Head nods and uh-huhs. Thumbs-ups can be common here.

2. **DIRECT EXPRESSIONS OF UNDERSTANDING.** "I agree" or "That's a very good point."

3. **PARAPHRASING.** "So if I understand correctly, you're saying . . ."

4. **APOLOGIES, GRATITUDE, AND THEIR ACCEPTANCE.** "I'm sorry" or "Thank you so much!" "It's okay" or "You're welcome."

5. **SENTENCE FINISHING, POSITIVE.**

Whining functions to make what might otherwise be an ordinary complaint into a plaintive or pleading form of emotional protest.

1. **VOCAL QUALITY.** High-pitched, nasal, sing-songy, or otherwise plaintive. For example, the question "why" might be expressed in a high-pitched voice and drawn out with an exaggerated "eeee" sound at the end, as in "whyyyyeeee?"

Emotional Labor Focus Group Interview Script

Guilt

Consultants often mention feeling guilty at times over some of their practices in the center. Were there times that you've felt guilty and why? How has such guilt affected you?

Emotional Intelligence

What are some ways you attempt to be mindful of your emotional state while in the writing center? How do you work—if at all—on perceiving your own emotions? Has anything in your writing center training or experience helped you to refine this ability?

What are some ways you attempt to regulate—if at all—your emotional state while in the writing center? Has anything in your writing center training or experience helped you to refine this ability?

In what ways—if at all—do you attempt to observe others' emotional states in the writing center? What things do you pick up on in sessions? What (if anything) in your training or experience in the center has contributed to your ability to perceive others' emotional states?

https://doi.org/10.7330/9781646428649.c008

In what ways—if at all—do you attempt to regulate or manage others' emotional states in the writing center? What emotions or situations do you try to manage in sessions? What (if anything) in your training or experience in the center has contributed to your ability to regulate or manage others' emotional states?

Emotional Dissonance (Surface Acting)

Are there times when you feel you have to put on a "mask" in order to express what you perceive to be the right emotions for the job? What are those times, and why?

In what situations might you display emotions at the Writing Center that you aren't actually feeling? Why?

When working with writers, in what situations might you behave differently than how you feel? Why?

Emotional Effort (Deep Acting)

When at work, do you try to actually experience the emotions that you think you're supposed to show with writers? How so? When is this easier than at other times?

When working with writers, do you attempt to create certain emotions in yourself that present what you think is the preferred image of the writing center? Why or why not? What do you perceive that image to be? If you do create emotions, how would you describe them?

Emotional Exhaustion

When over the course of a shift are you most likely to feel drained or burned out? Why do you think that is?

When over the course of a semester are you most likely to feel drained or burned out? Why do you think that is?

Depersonalization

Are there times when you feel you begin to treat writers impersonally? When is this more likely to occur and why?

Do you feel the job has hardened you emotionally or made you more empathetic? How so?

Personal Accomplishment

Do you feel that you can fairly easily understand how your session partners feel about things? How so?

Do you feel capable of creating a relaxed atmosphere for writers at the center? How so?

What are some of your personal accomplishments in your work at the center? What are you proud of in your work here and why?

Job Satisfaction

Overall, would you say you are satisfied working at the center? Why or why not?

References

Adler-Kassner, L. (2008). *The activist WPA: Changing stories about writing and writers.* Utah State University Press.

Adler-Kassner, L., & Wardle, E. (2015). *Naming what we know: Threshold concepts of writing studies.* Utah State University Press.

Ahmed, S. (2004). Affective economies. *Social Text, 79*(2), 117–139.

Alcorn, M. (2002). *Changing the subject in English class: Discourse and the constructions of desire.* Southern Illinois University Press.

Alemdar, M., & Anilan, H. (2022). Reflection of social capital in educational processes: Emotional literacy and emotional labor context. *Asia Pacific Education Review, 23*(1), 27–43.

Arrizabalaga, J., Boddice, R., Fernández-Fontecha, L., Hutchison, E., Nagy, P., Rosón, M., & Vidor, G. M. (2019). *Emotional bodies: The historical performativity of emotions.* University of Illinois Press.

Austin, E. J., Saklofske, D. H., Smith, M., & Tohver, G. (2014). Associations of the managing the emotions of others (MEOS) scale with personality, the Dark Triad and trait EI. *Personality and Individual Differences, 65,* 8–13.

Babcock, J. C., & Banks, J. C. (2019). Interobserver agreement and the effects of ethnicity on observational coding of affect. *Journal of Social and Personal Relationships, 36*(9), 2842–2856.

Babcock, R. D., & Thonus, T. (2012). *Researching the writing center: Towards an evidence-based practice.* Peter Lang International Academic Publishers.

https://doi.org/10.7330/9781646428649.c009

Bakhtin, M. (1986). The problem of speech genres. In C. Emerson & M. Holquist (Eds.), *Speech genres and other late essays* (V. McGee, Trans.; pp. 60–102). University of Texas Press.

Banks, J. C. (2018). *The effects of ethnicity on the cross-cultural reliability of the specific affect coding system* [Doctoral dissertation, University of Houston].

Bawarshi, A. (2000). The genre function. *College English, 62*(3), 335–360.

Beaufort, A. (2007). *College writing and beyond: A new framework for university writing instruction.* Utah State University Press, 2007.

Beck, J. (2018, November 26). The concept creep of "emotional labor." *The Atlantic.*

Benesch, S. (2012). *Considering emotions in critical English language teaching: Theories and praxis.* Routledge.

Ben-Ze'ev, A. (2001). *The subtlety of emotions.* MIT Press.

Black, L. J. (1998). *Between talk and teaching: Reconsidering the writing conference.* Utah State University Press.

Bolger, N., DeLongis, A., Kessler, R. C., & Wethington, E. (1989). The contagion of stress across multiple roles. *Journal of Marriage and the Family, 51*(1), 175–183.

Boyd, K. (2021). The surface act: Exercising emotional intelligence as a filter of racial awareness as a means of survival at PWIs. *The Vermont Connection, 42*(6), 52–60.

Brandt, D. (2001). *Literacy in American lives.* Cambridge University Press.

Brewer, M., & di Gennaro, K. (2018). Naming what we feel. *Composition Studies, 46*(2), 15–34.

Brody, N. (2004). What cognitive intelligence is and what emotional intelligence is not. *Psychological Inquiry, 15*(3), 234–238.

Canning, E., Muenks, K., Green, D. J., & Murphy, M. C. (2019). STEM faculty who believe ability is fixed have larger racial achievement gaps and inspire less student motivation in their classes. *Science Advances, 5*(2). https://advances.sciencemag.org /content/5/2/eaau4734?utm_source=15-faculty-minds

Carino, P. (2001). Reading our own words: Rhetorical analysis and the institutional discourse of writing centers. In P. Gillespie, A. Gillam, L. Falls Brown & B. Stay (Eds.), *Writing center research: Extending the conversation* (pp. 91–110). Routledge.

Carino, P. (2003). Power and authority in peer tutoring. In M. Pemberton & J. Kinkaid (Eds.), *The center will hold: Critical perspectives on writing center scholarship* (pp. 96–113). Utah State University Press.

Caswell, N., Grutsch McKinney, J., & Jackson, R. (2016). *The working lives of new writing center directors.* Utah State University Press, 2016.

Chamorro-Premuzic, T., & Yearsley, A. (2017, January 12). The downsides of being very emotionally intelligent. *Harvard Business Review.* https://hbr.org/2017/01/the -downsides-of-being-very-emotionally-intelligent

Chandler, S. (2007). Fear, teaching composition, and students' discursive choices: Re-thinking connections between emotions and college student writing. *Composition Studies, 35*(2), 53–70.

Chang, M. (2009). An appraisal perspective of teacher burnout: Examining the emotional work of teachers. *Educational Psychology Review, 21*(3), 193–218.

Chavannes, N., Cole, M., Guido, J., & Louissaint, S. (2022). Navigating emotions and interpersonal relations in graduate administrative writing center work. In J. Morris & K. Concannon (Eds.), *Emotions and affect in writing centers* (pp. 65–81). Parlor Press.

Chu, K. H., Baker, M. A., & Murrmann, S. K. (2021). When we are onstage, we smile: The effects of emotional labor on employee work outcomes. *International Journal of Hospitality Management, 31*(3), 906–915.

Clark, C. T., Chrisman, A., & Lewis, S. G. (2022). (Un)Standardizing emotions: An ethical critique of social and emotional learning standards. *Teachers College Record, 124*(7), 131–149.

Clark, I. L. (1988). Collaboration and ethics in writing center pedagogy. *The Writing Center Journal, 9*(1), 3–12.

Coan, J. A., & Gottman, J. M. (2007). The specific affect coding system (SPAFF). In J. A. Coan & J. B. Allen (Eds.), *Handbook of emotion elicitation and assessment* (pp. 267–285). Oxford University Press.

Coe, R., Lingard, L., & Teslenko, T. (Eds.). (2002). *The rhetoric and ideology of genre: Strategies for stability and change.* Hampton Press.

Cole, K., & Hassel, H. (Eds.). (2017). *Surviving sexism in academia: Strategies for feminist leadership.* Routledge.

Corbett, S. J. (2011). Using case study multi-methods to investigate close(r) collaboration: Tutoring and the directive/nondirective instructional continuum. *The Writing Center Journal, 31*(1), 55–81.

Corbett, S. J. (2013). Negotiating pedagogical authority: The rhetoric of writing center tutoring styles and methods. *Rhetoric Review, 32*(1), 81–98.

Costello, K. M. (2021). Naming and negotiating the emotional labors of writing center tutoring. In G. Giaimo (Ed.), *Wellness and care in writing center work.* Pressbooks. https://ship.pressbooks.pub/writingcentersandwellness/chapter/title-here/

Côté, S., Decelles, K., McCarthy, J., Van Kleef, G., & Hideg, I. (2011). The Jekyll and Hyde of emotional intelligence: Emotion-regulation knowledge facilitates both prosocial and interpersonally deviant behavior. *Psychological Science, 22*(8), 1073–1080.

Daniels, A. K. (1987). Invisible work. *Social problems, 34*(5), 403–415.

Davies, L. J., (2017). Grief and the new WPA. *WPA: Writing Program Administration, 40*(2), 40–51.

Devitt, A. (2014). Genre pedagogies. In G. Tate, A. R. Taggart, K. Schick & H. B. Hessler (Eds.), *A guide to composition pedagogies* (pp. 146–162). Oxford University Press.

Dixon, E. (2017). Strategy-centered or student-centered: A meditation on conflation. *WLN: A Journal of Writing Center Scholarship, 42*(3–4), 7–15.

D'Mello, S. K., Lehman, B., & Person, N. (2010). Monitoring affect during effortful problem solving activities. *International Journal of Artificial Intelligence in Education, 20,* 361–389.

Downs, D. (2020). Rhetoric: Making sense of human interaction and meaning-making. In E. Wardle & D. Downs (Eds.), *Writing about writing* (pp. 369–395). Bedford/St. Martin's.

Driscoll, D. L., & Powell, R. (2016). States, traits, and dispositions: The impact of emotion on writing development and writing transfer across college courses and beyond. *Composition Forum, 34.*

Driscoll, D. L., & Wells, J. (2020). Tutoring the whole person: Supporting emotional development in writers and tutors. *Praxis, 17*(3), 16–28.

Economic Policy Institute. (2026, January 16). *The productivity pay gap.* EPI. https://www.epi.org/productivity-pay-gap/

Faison, W., & Treviño, A. (2017). Race, retention, language, and literacy: The hidden curriculum of the writing center. *Peer Review, 1*(2).

Feez, S. (2002). Heritage and innovation in second language education. In A. M. Johns (Ed.), *Genre in the classroom: multiple perspectives* (pp. 43–69). Lawrence Erlbaum Associates.

Fleckenstein, K. (2003). *Embodied literacies: Imageword and a poetics of teaching.* Southern Illinois University Press.

Freedman, A. (1994). "Do as I say": The relationship between teaching and learning new genres. In A. Freedman & P. Medway (Eds.), *Genre and the new rhetoric* (pp. 191–210). Taylor & Francis.

Garrett, B., Landrum-Geyer, D., & Palmeri, J. (2012). *Re-inventing invention: A performance in three acts.* Computers and Composition Digital Press, Utah State University Press. The New Work of Composing. https://ccdigitalpress.org/book/nwc/chapters/garrett-et-al/

Gerber, L. G. (2014). *The rise and decline of faculty governance: Professionalization and the modern American university.* Johns Hopkins University Press.

Giaimo, G. (2023). *Unwell writing centers: Searching for wellness in neoliberal institutions and beyond.* Utah State University Press.

Giaimo, G. (2024). "I don't know how to feel": Unpacking emotion, affect, and educator burnout in a writing classroom during times of crisis. *Composition Studies, 52*(1). 69–88.

Giaimo, G., & Lawson, D. (2024). *Storying writing center labor for anti-capitalist futures.* WAC Clearinghouse.

Giese-Davis, J., Piemme, K. A., Dillon, C., & Twirbutt, S. (2005). Macrovariables in affective expression in women with breast cancer participating in support groups. In J. A. Harrigan, R. Rosenthal & K. R. Scherer (Eds.), *The new handbook of methods in nonverbal behavior research* (pp. 399–445). Oxford University Press.

Gilewicz, M., & Thonus, T. (2003). Close vertical transcription in writing center training and research. *Writing Center Journal, 24*(1), pp. 25–49.

Ginsberg, B. (2011). *The fall of the faculty.* Oxford University Press.

Godbee, B., Ozias, M., & Tang, J. K. (2015). Body + power + justice: Movement-based workshops for critical tutor education. *The Writing Center Journal, 34*(2), 61–112.

Goldblatt, E. (2007). *Because we live here: Sponsoring literacy beyond the college curriculum.* Hampton Press.

Goleman, D. (1995). *Emotional Intelligence.* Bantam.

Gottfredson, M. R., & Hirschi, T. (1990). *A general theory of crime.* Stanford University Press.

Grandey, A. A. (2000). Emotional regulation in the workplace: A new way to conceptualize emotional labor. *Journal of Occupational Health Psychology, 5*(1), 95–110.

Greenfield, L. (2019). *Radical writing center praxis: A paradigm for ethical political engagement.* Utah State University Press.

Greenfield, L., & Rowan, K. (Eds.). (2011). *Writing centers and the new racism: A call for sustainable dialogue and change.* University Press of Colorado.

Grieve, R., March, E., & Van Doorn, G. (2019). Masculinity might be more toxic than we think: The influence of gender roles on trait emotional manipulation. *Personality and Individual Differences, 138,* 157–162.

Grimm, N. M. (2011). Rhetheorizing writing center work to transform a system of advantage based on race. In L. Greenfield and K. Rowan (Eds.), *Writing centers and the new racism* (pp. 75–100). University Press of Colorado.

Haltiwanger Morrison, T. M., & Nanton, T. O. (2019). Dear writing centers: Black women speaking silence into language and action. *The Peer Review: Defining Welcome, 3.* https://thepeerreview-iwca.org/issues/redefining-welcome/dear-writing-centers-black-women-speaking-silence-into-language-and-action/

Hardt, M., & Negri, A. (2005). *Multitude: War and democracy in the age of empire.* Penguin.

Hargreaves, A., & Tucker, E. (1991). Teaching and guilt: Exploring the feelings of teaching. *Teaching and Teacher Education, 7,* 491–505.

Harms, P. D., & Credé, M. (2010). Emotional intelligence and transformational and transactional leadership: A meta-analysis. *Journal of Leadership & Organizational Studies, 17*(1), 5–17.

Harris, L. C., & Ogbonna, E. (2002). Exploring service sabotage: The antecedents, types and consequences of frontline, deviant, antiservice behaviors. *Journal of Service Research, 4*(3), 163–183.

Harris, M. (1986). *Teaching one-to-one: The writing conference.* NCTE.

Harris, M. (1995). Talking in the middle: Why writers need writing tutors. *College English, 57*(1), 27–42.

Harris, M. (2010). Making our institutional discourse sticky: Suggestions for effective rhetoric. *The Writing Center Journal, 30*(2), 47–71.

Hemmeter, T. (1994). Live and on stage: Writing center stories and tutorial authority. *The Writing Center Journal, 15*(1), 35–50.

Herman, L., Herman, C. G., & Hinman, R. (2020). Diminishing power and authority through modes of dress: Toward a more equitable writing center. *The Peer Review, 4*(1). https://thepeerreview-iwca.org/issues/issue-4-1/diminishing-power-and-authority-through-modes-of-dress-toward-a-more-equitable-writing-center/

Herrnstein, R. & Murray, C. (1994). *The bell curve: Intelligence and class structure in American life.* Free Press.

Hobfoll, S., Halbesleben, J., Neveu, J., & Westman, M. (2018). Conservation of resources in the organizational context: The reality of resources and their consequences. *Annual Review of Organizational Psychology and Organizational Behavior, 5,* 103–128.

Hochschild, A. (2012). *The managed heart: Commercialization of human feeling.* University of California Press.

Hochschild, A. (2013). *So how's the family? And other essays.* University of California Press.

Holt, M., Anderson, L., & Rouzie, A. (2003). Making emotion work visible in writing program administration. In L. Micciche & D. Jacobs (Eds.), *A way to move: Rhetorics of emotion and composition studies* (pp. 147–160). Boynton/Cook.

Humphrey, R. H., Ashforth, B. E., & Diefendorff, J. M. (2015). The bright side of emotional labor. *Journal of Organizational Behavior, 36* (6), 749–769.

Iantorno, L. (2022). Positive affect display and emotional labor in the writing center: A qualitative study. In J. Morris & K. Concannon (Eds.), *Emotions and affect in writing centers* (pp. 199–216). Parlor Press.

Ilievová, L., Juhásová, I., & Baumgartner, F. (2013). Opportunities for emotional intelligence in the context of nursing. *Journal of Health Sciences, 3*(1), 20–25.

Jackson, R., McKinney, J. G., & Caswell, N. I. (2016). Writing center administration and/as emotional labor. *Composition Forum, 34.*

Johnson, M., Levy, D., Manthey, K., & Novotny, M. (2015). Embodiment: Embodying feminist rhetorics. *Peitho Journal, 18*(1), 39–44.

Jung, M. F. (2016). Coupling interactions and performance: Predicting team performance from thin slices of conflict. *ACM Transactions on Computer-Human Interaction (TOCHI), 23*(3), 1–32.

Kahan, D. M. (2013). Ideology, motivated reasoning, and cognitive reflection. *Judgment and Decision Making, 8*(4), 407–424.

Kilduff, M., Chiaburu, D., & Menges, J. (2010). Strategic use of emotional intelligence in organizational settings: Exploring the dark side. *Research in Organizational Behavior, 30,* 129–152.

Kjesrud, R. D. (2015). Lessons from data: Avoiding lore bias in research paradigms. *The Writing Center Journal, 34*(2), 33–58.

Kreber, C. (2009). Supporting student learning in the context of diversity, complexity, and uncertainty. In C. Kreber (ed.), *The university and its disciplines: Teaching and learning within and beyond disciplinary boundaries* (pp. 3–18). Routledge.

Kruml, S. M., & Geddes, D. (2000). Exploring the dimensions of emotional labor: The heart of Hochschild's work. *Management Communication Quarterly, 14*(1), 8–49.

Landy, F. J. (2005). Some historical and scientific issues related to research on emotional intelligence. *Journal of Organizational Behavior, 26*(4), 411–424.

Lape, N. (2008). Training tutors in emotional intelligence: Toward a pedagogy of empathy. *WLN: A Journal of Writing Center Scholarship, 33*(2), 1–6.

Lauer, J., & J. Asher. (1988). *Composition research: Empirical designs.* Oxford University Press.

Lawson, D. (2015). Metaphors and ambivalence: Affective dimensions in writing center studies. *WLN: A Journal of Writing Center Scholarship, 40*(3–4), 20–27.

Lee, J. J., & Ok, C. (2012). Reducing burnout and enhancing job satisfaction: Critical role of hotel employees' emotional intelligence and emotional labor. *International Journal of Hospitality Management, 31*(4), 1101–1112.

Lerner, N. (2019). Growing pains in the golden age. *College English, 81*(5), 457–466.

Lindquist, J. (2004). Class affects, classroom affectations: Working through the paradoxes of strategic empathy. *College English, 67*(2), 187–209.

Mackiewicz, J., & Thompson, I. (2013). Motivational scaffolding, politeness, and writing center tutoring. *The Writing Center Journal, 33*(1), 38–73.

Mackiewicz, J., & Thompson, I. (2018). *Talk about writing: The tutoring strategies of experienced writing center tutors.* Routledge.

Madriz, E. (2000). Focus groups in feminist research. In N. K. Denzin & Y. S. Lincoln (Eds.), *Handbook of qualitative research.* Sage.

Mannon, B. (2021). Centering the emotional labor of writing center tutors. *Writing Center Journal, 39*(1–2), 143–168.

Maslach C., & Leiter M. P. (2016). Understanding the burnout experience: Recent research and its implications for psychiatry. *World Psychiatry, 15*(2), 103–111.

Maslach, C., Schaufeli, W. B., & Leiter, M. P. (2001). Job burnout. *Annual Review of Psychology, 52*(1), 397–422.

Mattingly, M., Helakoski, C., Lundberg, C., & Walz, K. (2021). Cultivating an emotionally intelligent writing center culture online. In G. Giaimo & Y. Hashlamon (Eds.), *Wellness and care in writing center work.* Pressbooks.

Mayer, J. D. (2001). Emotion, intelligence, and emotional intelligence. In J. P. Forgas (Ed.), *Handbook of affect and social cognition* (pp. 410–431). Erlbaum.

McKinney, J. G. (2012). *Peripheral visions for writing centers.* Utah State University Press.

Mesmer-Magnus, J. R., DeChurch, L. A., & Wax, A. (2012). Moving emotional labor beyond surface and deep acting: A discordance–congruence perspective. *Organizational Psychology Review, 2*(1), 6–53.

Meyer, J. H., & Land, R. (2006). Threshold concepts and troublesome knowledge: Issues of liminality. In J. H. Meyer & R. Land (Eds.), *Overcoming barriers to student understanding* (pp. 19–32). Routledge.

Micciche, L. R. (2002). More than a feeling: Disappointment and WPA work. *College English, 64*(4), 432–458.

Micciche, L. R. (2007). *Doing emotion: Rhetoric, writing, teaching.* Heinemann.

Miller, C. R. (1984). Genre as social action. *Quarterly Journal of Speech, 70*(2), 151–167.

Mischel, W. (1974). Processes in delay of gratification. *Advances in Experimental Social Psychology, 7,* 249–292.

Morris, J., & Concannon, K. (Eds.). (2022). *Emotions and affect in writing centers.* Parlor Press.

Morris, J. A., & Feldman, D. C. (1996). The dimensions, antecedents, and consequences of emotional labor. *Academy of Management Review, 21*(4), 986–1010.

Murensky, C. L. (2000). The relationships between emotional intelligence, personality, critical thinking ability and organizational leadership performance at upper levels of management [Doctoral dissertation, George Mason University]. PsyNET. https://www.proquest.com/docview/304670322?pq-origsite=gscholar&fromopenview=true&sourcetype=Dissertations%20&%20Theses

Nagler, U. K., Reiter, K. J., Furtner, M. R., & Rauthmann, J. F. (2014). Is there a "dark intelligence"? Emotional intelligence is used by dark personalities to emotionally manipulate others. *Personality and Individual Differences, 65*, 47–52.

Napoleone, A. R. (2019). Class division, class affect, and the role of the writing center in literacy practices. In H. Denny, R. Mundy, L. M. Naydan, R. Sévère & A. Sicari (Eds.), *Out in the center: Public controversies and private struggles* (pp. 203–211). Utah State University Press.

National Center for Education Statistics (NCES). (n.d.) *Average undergraduate tuition, fees, room, and board rates charged for full-time students in degree-granting postsecondary institutions, by level and control of institution: Selected academic years, 1963–64 through 2021–22.* Retrieved November 1, 2023, from https://nces.ed.gov/programs/digest/d22/tables/dt22_330.10.asp

Navickas, K. (2020). The emotional labor of becoming: Lessons from the exiting writing center director. In C. A. Wooten, J. Babb, K. M. Costello & K. Navickas (Eds.), *The things we carry: Strategies for recognizing and negotiating emotional labor in writing program administration* (pp. 56–74). Utah State University Press.

Navickas, K., Costello, K. M., & Simpson-Farrow, T. (2022). Tales of becoming and letting go: The emotional labor and identities of writing center administrators in transition. In J. Morris & K. Concannon (Eds.), *Emotions and affect in writing centers.* WAC Clearinghouse.

Nicklay, J. (2012). Got guilt? Consultant guilt in the writing center community. *The Writing Center Journal, 32*(1), 14–27.

Nightingale, S., Spiby, H., Sheen, K., & Slade, P. (2018). The impact of emotional intelligence in health care professionals on caring behaviour towards patients in clinical and long-term care settings: Findings from an integrative review. *International Journal of Nursing Studies, 80*, 106–117.

North, S. M. (1984). The idea of a writing center. *College English, 46*(5), 433–446.

North, S. M. (1994). Revisiting "The idea of a writing center." *The Writing Center Journal, 15*(1), 7–19.

Nozaki, Y., & Koyasu, M. (2013). The relationship between trait emotional intelligence and interaction with ostracized others' retaliation. *PLOS One, 8*(10), 1–7.

Nyhan, B., & Reifler, J. (2010). When corrections fail: The persistence of political misperceptions. *Political Behavior, 32*(2), 303–330.

Pemberton, M. (1992). The prison, the hospital, and the madhouse: Redefining metaphors for the writing center. *Writing Lab Newsletter, 17*(1), 11–16.

Penprase, B., Oakley, B., Ternes, R., & Driscoll, D. (2015). Do higher dispositions for empathy predispose males toward careers in nursing? A descriptive correlational design. *Nursing Forum, 50*(1), 1–8.

Perry, A. (2016). Training for triggers: Helping writing center consultants navigate emotional sessions. *Composition Forum, 34*.

Peterson, R. (2023). Conversation shaper: Emotional intelligence as a teachable skill: How empathy-based training can shape the writing center into an activist space. *The Peer Review, 7*(2). https://thepeerreview-iwca.org/issues/issue-7-2/conversation

-shaper-emotional-intelligence-as-a-teachable-skill-how-empathy-based-training
-can-shape-the-writing-center-into-an-activist-space/

Prawat, R., Byers, J., & Anderson, A. H. (1983). An attributional analysis of teachers' affective reactions to student success and failure. *American Educational Research Journal, 20*, 137–152.

Richmond, K. (2002). Repositioning emotions in composition studies. *Composition Studies, 30*(1), 67–82.

Rickert, T. J. (2007). *Acts of enjoyment: Rhetoric, Žižek, and the return of the subject.* University of Pittsburgh Press.

Ritchie, J., Lewis, J., Nicholls, C. M., & Ormston, R. (2003). *Qualitative research practice* (Vol. 757). Sage.

Ritter, K. (2011). "What would happen if everybody behaved as I do?": May Bush, Randall Jarrell, and the historical 'disappointment' of women WPAs. *Composition Studies, 39*(1), 13–39.

Roberts, R. D., Zeidner, M., & Matthews, G. (2001). Does emotional intelligence meet traditional standards for an intelligence? Some new data and conclusions. *Emotion, 1*(3), 196–231.

Robillard, A. E. (2007). We won't get fooled again: On the absence of angry responses to plagiarism in composition studies. *College English, 70*(1), 10–31.

Ryan, L., & Zimmerelli, L. (2016). *The Bedford guide for writing tutors.* Bedford/ St. Martins.

Salovey, P., & Mayer, J. D. (1990). *Emotional intelligence. Imagination, Cognition, and Personality, 9*(3), 185–211.

Schein, E. (2017). *Organizational culture and leadership.* Jossey-Bass.

Sévère, R. (2019). Black male bodies in the center. In H. Denny, R. Mundy, L. M. Naydan, R. Sévère & A. Sicari (Eds), *Out in the center: Public controversies and private struggles* (pp. 43–50). Utah State University Press.

Shamoon, L. K., & Burns, D. H. (1995). A critique of pure tutoring. *The Writing Center Journal, 15*(2), 134–151.

Simmons, E., Miller, L. K., Prendergast, C., & McGuigan, C. (2020). Is tutoring stressful?: Measuring tutors' cortisol levels. *WLN: A Journal of Writing Center Scholarship, 44*(5–6), 18–26.

Sloterdijk, P. (1987). *Critique of cynical reason.* University of Minnesota Press.

Smith, S. (1997). The genre of the end comment: Conventions in teacher responses to student writing. *College Composition and Communication, 48*(2), 249–268.

Smithson, J. (2008). Focus groups. In P. Alasuutari, L. Bickman & J. Brannen (Eds.), *The Sage handbook of social research methods* (pp. 357–370). Sage.

Spencer, S., & Rupp, D. E. (2009). Angry, guilty, and conflicted: Injustice toward coworkers heightens emotional labor through cognitive and emotional mechanisms. *Journal of Applied Psychology, 94*, 429–444.

Staub, M. E. (2016). Controlling ourselves: Emotional intelligence, the marshmallow test, and the inheritance of race. *American Studies, 55*(1), 59–80.

Stenberg, S. (2011). Teaching and (re)learning the rhetoric of emotion. *Pedagogy, 11*(2), 349–369.

Street, B. (2006). Autonomous and ideological models of literacy: Approaches from new literacy studies. *Media Anthropology Network, 17*(1), 1–15.

Sura, T., Wells, J. M., Schoen, M., Elder, C., & Driscoll, D. L. (2009). Praxis and allies: The WPA board game. *WPA: Writing Program Administration, 32*(3).

Thompson, I., & Mackiewicz, J. (2014). Questioning in writing center conferences. *The Writing Center Journal, 33*(2), 37–70.

Towle, B. (2019). Other people's houses: Identity and service in writing center work. In H. Denny, R. Mundy, L. M. Naydan, R. Sévère & A. Sicari (Eds), *Out in the center: Public controversies and private struggles* (pp. 197–202). Utah State University Press.

Travis, D. J., & Thorpe-Moscon, J. (2018). Day-to-day experiences of emotional tax among men and women of colour in the workplace. *Catalyst.* https://www.catalyst.org/wpcontent/uploads/2019/02/emotionaltax.pdf

Wardle, E. (2019, January 30). You know more than you think you do about writing. *Inside Higher Ed.* https://www.insidehighered.com/blogs/just-visiting/guest-post-you-know-more-you-think-about-teaching-writing

Waugh, C. E., & Fredrickson, B. L. (2006). Nice to know you: Positive emotions, self–other overlap, and complex understanding in the formation of a new relationship. *The Journal of Positive Psychology, 1*(2), 93–106.

Webster, T. (2021). Queerly centered: LGBTQA writing center directors navigate the workplace. Utah State University Press.

Welch, N. (1995). Migrant rationalities: Graduate students and the idea of authority in the writing center. *The Writing Center Journal, 16*(1), 5–23.

Westman, M. (2001). Stress and strain crossover. *Human Relations, 54*(6), 717–751.

Wilson, J. Q., & Herrnstein, R. J. (1985). *Crime and human nature.* Simon and Schuster.

Wooten, C., Babb, J., Costello, K. M., & Navickas, K. (2020). *The things we carry: Strategies for recognizing and negotiating emotional labor in writing program administration.* Utah State University Press.

Yun-Tsan, L., & Yi-Chih, T. (2017). Influence of emotional labor and emotional intelligence on service sabotage. *Advances in Management, 10*(8), 1–9.

Zapf, D. (2002). Emotion work and psychological well-being: A review of the literature and some conceptual considerations. *Human Resource Management Review, 12*(2), 237–268.

Index

Adler-Kassner, Linda, 117
affect, vs. emotion, 13–15. *See also* deep acting; emotional labor; Specific Affect Coding System (SPAFF); surface acting
Affection (SPAFF code), 25, 28, 31, 34, 37–39, 48–55, 57–58, 99–101, 137; as counterindicator, 132, 133, 135; full code, 123–124
Ahmed, Sara, 7, 14, 111
Alcorn, Marshall, 116
Alemdar, Melek, 97–98
alienation, 19, 73, 84
Amy (case study), 47–51, 55–59. *See also* James (case study)
Anger (SPAFF code), 25, 31, 99, 101, 107, 137; as counterindicator, 125, 128; full code, 124–125
Anilan, Huseyin, 97–98
Arrizabalaga, Jon, 40
Asher, Janice, 34
authority (tutoring), 42 60

Babcock, Rebecca, 22
backchanneling (validation indicator), 30, 33, 35–41, 43, 49–57, 67, 99, 103–107; as counterindicator, 133, 134, 135; as indicator, 134–135, 140

Bakhtin, Mikhail, 16, 89–90, 98
Bawarshi, Anis, 109–110
Bedford Guide for Writing Tutors, The, 4–6, 46, 59
Beldoch, Michael, 90
Belligerence/Contempt (SPAFF code), 25, 27, 31, 33, 124, 125–126, 138; as counterindicator, 126–129, 132–133, 135, 138
Ben-ze'ev, Aaron, 76
Blackness, black culture, 96
body language, 30–31, 81, 98, 102–108, 123–124, 137
Bolger, Niall, 72
Boyd, Khadija, 95–96
Brandt, Deborah, 108
Brewer, Meaghan, 9
Burns, Deborah, 42
burnout, 18–19, 61–88, 111–112; emotional exhaustion, 62, 64–66, 73, 77, 81, 86, 142

Canning, Elizabeth, 115
Carino, Steven, 42
Caswell, Nicole, 10
Chang, Mei-Lin, 64, 77
Chavennes, Nicole, 11
Clark, Caroline, 96

closed-ended questions, 39, 44, 48–49, 55
Coan, James, 18, 24–28, 37–38, 104–105, 123–135
Coe, Richard, 106
cognitive dissonance, 113
collaboration codes, 43–46
Concannon, Kelly, 11, 33
Contempt (SPAFF code). *See* Belligerence/
  Contempt
content-clarifying questions, 44, 104
Corbett, Steven, 43–45, 55
Criticism (SPAFF code), 25, 31, 38, 101, 138; full
  code, 126; as counterindicator, 127
cynicism (burnout), 19, 61–88, 93, 112

Daniels, Arlene Kaplan, 21, 119
deep acting (emotional exertion, EE), 12–15,
  19, 64–67, 70–72, 83–87, 107, 142
Defensiveness (SPAFF code), 25, 31, 50, 53–54,
  100–101, 104–105, 107, 119, 127, 138; as counterindicator, 124, 127, 135
depersonalization (burnout), 65–66, 73, 75–77,
  84–86, 142
Devitt, Amy, 99
di Gennaro, Kristen, 9
directive questions, 44, 55–57
directive/nondirective continuum, 42–45,
  56–59, 63, 107
Disgust (SPAFF code), 25, 31, 100, 138; full
  code, 128
diversity, equity, and inclusion (DEI), 87,
  117–118. *See also* linguistic hegemony;
  neurodiversity
Dixon, Elise, 62–63, 77
Domineering/Threats (SPAFF code), 25–27, 32,
  49, 53–54, 99–100, 103–105, 107, 128–129, 139;
  as counterindicator, 127, 128, 133, 135
Driscoll, Dana, 91

Economic Policy Institute, 8
embodiment, genre, 10, 15–17, 40, 56, 92, 103,
  106–107; rhetoric, 16–17
emotional dissonance. *See* surface acting
emotional exertion. *See* deep acting
emotional intelligence (EI), 11, 18–19, 27, 47, 57,
  59, 64–65, 73, 78, 86–88, 89–90, 141; critiques
  of EI via racialized habitus, 93–97; and cynicism, 80–85; dark side (of EI), 19, 92–93; EI
  writing center research, 90–91; emotional
  literacy (vs. EI), 97–99
emotional labor: concept creep, 11–12; toll of,
  6, 19, 61, 79, 112; vs. emotion work, 10–11; as
  metalabor, 119–120. *See also* deep acting;
  surface acting

emotional tax (identity), 66
emotional turn, 121
empathy (indicator of Affection), 50, 52, 101,
  124, 137
Enthusiasm (SPAFF code), 25, 31, 37, 39, 49–54,
  99, 139; full code, 129–130

faculty development, 112, 117
Faison, Wonderful, 96
Fear/Tension (SPAFF code), 25, 32, 37, 49, 54,
  64, 101; as counterindicator, 131, 132, 133; full
  code, 130, 139
feeling rules (Hochschild), 6–7, 20, 61–64
fixed mindset, 115
Fleckenstein, Kristie, 15
focus groups (tutor testimonies), 19, 64–67
Freedman, Aviva, 99

Garrett, Bre, 15
Geddes, Deanna, 12
genre critique, 92, 99; genre, secondary, 16,
  89–90, 98
Gerber, Harry, 8
Giese-Davis, Janine, 27
Ginsberg, Benjamin, 8
Giaimo, Genie, 21, 28, 40, 85, 96, 113, 119–121
Gilewicz, Magdalena, 44
Goldblatt, Eli, 108
Goleman, Daniel, 90, 92, 94
Gottfredson, Michael, 95
Gottman, John, 18, 24–28, 37–38, 104–105,
  123–135
Grandey, Alicia, 12
Greenfield, Laura, 79, 118
Grieve, Rachel, 93
Grimm, Nancy, 79, 115
guilt (tutor), 61–88, 141

habitus, 88, 92–93, 96–97, 99, 106–107
Haltiwanger Morrison, Talisha, 96
Hardt, Michael, 14
Harris, Muriel, 43, 113
Harris, Lloyd, 63
Herrnstein, Richard, 95
Hirschi, Travis, 95
Hobfell, Stevan, 71, 79
Hochschild, Arlie, 6–15, 19–20, 23, 39–41, 46, 62,
  75, 86, 109, 121
Holt, Mara, 11
Humor (SPAFF code), 25, 32, 37, 39, 41, 48,
  51–54, 57–58, 139; as counterindicator, 31,
  125, 129, 131, 138; full code, 131–132

Iantorno, Luke, 91
imperatives (collaboration code), 45, 51, 55–57, 103–104
imposter syndrome, 62
Interest (SPAFF code), 25, 32, 37–39, 52–54, 58, 99, 101, 104, 120, 139; as counterindicator, 130; full code, 132–133
interruptions (collaboration code), 43–44, 53
intersectionality, 10, 28, 66, 88, 101, 115
invisible work, 10, 21, 119–120

James (case study), 47–51, 53–60
joint productions (collaboration code), 43–44

Kaplan Daniels, Arlene. *See* Daniels, Arlene Kaplan
Kaylee (case study), 48–60
Kilduff, Martin, 92
Koyasu, Masuo, 93
Kruml, Susan, 12

Land, Ray, 117
Lape, Noreen, 90
Lauer, J. William, 34
Lawson, Daniel, 23, 113, 119–120
Lawrence (case study), 48–60
Lee, JungHoon, 13, 19, 65, 73, 75, 86–87
Leiter, Michael, 61
Lerner, Neal, 89
libidinal investments, 116
linguistic hegemony, 115, 120
literacy, autonomous model of, 114–116
literacy sponsorship, 108

Mackiewicz, Jo, 38, 41, 67, 89
main channel overlaps, 44, 49
Mannon, Bethany, 10, 20–21, 23, 27, 40, 43, 58–59, 120
marshmallow test (Mischel/self-control), 94
Maslach, Christina, 61
Mattingly, Miranda, 11, 91
Mayer, John, 94
McAuley, William, 109
McKinney, Jackie Grutsch, 9
metalabor, 119–120
"metatalk," 82, 86
Meyer, Jan, 117
Micciche, Laura, 15, 40
microaggressions, 9, 40, 107
Miller, Carolyn, 16–17
mindfulness (self-care), 17, 47, 109
Mischel, Walter, 94
Morris, Janine, 11, 33

Murray, Charles, 95
Murray Costello, Kristi, 11

Nanton, Talia, 96
Napoleone, Anna Rita, 11, 14–15
Navickas, Kate, 11
Negri, Antonio, 14
neurodiversity, 28, 69
Nicklay, Jennifer, 62–63, 77
nondirective tutoring. *See* directive/nondirective continuum
Nozaki, Yuki, 93

Ogbonna, Emmanuel, 63
Ok, Chihyung, 13, 19, 65, 73, 75, 86–87
open-ended questions, 4, 32, 43–46, 49, 55, 132

Peterson, Rachel, 91
pleasure activism, 121
positionality, 16, 21, 118–119
Powell, Roger, 91
proxemics (workshop), 103–104

qualifiers (collaboration code), 45, 52, 55–58

race, 28, 66, 79, 100–101, 106, 112, 115–117; and EI, 93–95, 38
rapport, 3–5, 28, 30–31, 35, 45, 48, 52, 57–59, 83, 101, 123, 137
regulation, emotional, 19, 83, 89–90, 96
Rickert, Thomas, 84
Ritchie, Jane, 65
Rowan, Karen, 79

Sadness (SPAFF code), 25, 32, 64, 99, 139; full code, 133; as counterindicator, 134
Salovey, Peter, 94
scaffolding, 22, 38, 41, 44, 67–68, 72, 76, 84, 89, 98
Schein, Edgar, 91
self-awareness (EI), 19, 90
self-care, 109
self-efficacy (tutors), 3, 68, 73
Sévère, Richard, 10, 16, 106
Shamoon, Linda, 42
Sloterdijk, Peter, 83
Smithson, Janet, 65
"Statement on Students' Right to Their Own Language," 118
Stonewalling (SPAFF code), 25, 33, 101, 140; as counterindicator, 131–133; full code, 133–134
Specific Affect Coding System (SPAFF), 15, 23–24, 26; adaptation for writing center,

18–19, 26–34, 36–41; cultural informant approach, 26, 34; protocol, 29
Staub, Michael, 93–97
Street, Brian, 114
Smith, Summer, 16
surface acting (emotional dissonance), 12–13, 19, 48, 61, 63, 65–73, 77, 83–86, 107, 142

Tension (SPAFF). *See* fear/tension
Thompson, Isabelle, 38, 41, 67, 89
Thonus, Terese, 22, 44
Thorpe-Moscon, Jennifer, 66
threshold concepts, 8, 117–118
Towle, Beth, 11
Travis, Dnika, 66
Treviño, Anna, 96

unrelated questions (collaboration code), 45, 55

Validation (SPAFF code), 25, 30, 32–33, 36–41, 43, 46, 51–54, 57–59, 99, 101, 103–104, 140; as counterindicator, 33, 128, 132, 134, 139–140; full code, 134–135. *See also* backchanneling
vertical transcription, 30, 66

Wardle, Elizabeth, 9, 117
Webster, Travis, 11
Wells, Jennifer, 91
Whining (SPAFF code), 25, 33, 140; full code, 135

Yi-Chih, Tsi, 12
Yun-Tsan, Lin, 12

About the Author

Daniel Lawson is a professor of English at Central Michigan University, where he serves as the writing center director. He has published on rhetoric, media studies, and writing centers. He is the coauthor of *Storying Writing Center Labor for Anti-Capitalist Futures* with Genie Giaimo. His writing center work has appeared in venues such as *WLN*, *Praxis*, *The Peer Review*, and *The Learning Assistance Review*. He has served as the president of the Michigan Writing Centers Association and as an at-large board member of the East Central Writing Centers Association.

www.ingramcontent.com/pod-product-compliance
Ingram Content Group UK Ltd.
Pitfield, Milton Keynes, MK11 3LW, UK
UKHW041841150726
7214IPUK00015B/108